Distraction

THE ART OF LIVING SERIES

Series Editor: Mark Vernon

From Plato to Bertrand Russell philosophers have engaged wide audiences on matters of life and death. *The Art of Living* series aims to open up philosophy's riches to a wider public once again. Taking its lead from the concerns of the ancient Greek philosophers, the series asks the question "How should we live?". Authors draw on their own personal reflections to write philosophy that seeks to enrich, stimulate and challenge the reader's thoughts about their own life.

Clothes *John Harvey*
Commitment *Piers Benn*
Death *Todd May*
Deception *Ziyad Marar*
Distraction *Damon Young*
Faith *Theo Hobson*
Fame *Mark Rowlands*
Forgiveness *Eve Garrard and David McNaughton*
Hunger *Raymond Tallis*
Illness *Havi Carel*
Me *Mel Thompson*
Middle Age *Christopher Hamilton*
Money *Eric Lonergan*
Pets *Erica Fudge*
Science *Steve Fuller*
Sport *Colin McGinn*
Wellbeing *Mark Vernon*
Work *Lars Svendsen*

Distraction

Damon Young

ACUMEN

© Damon Young, 2008, 2010

This book is copyright under the Berne Convention.
No reproduction without permission.
All rights reserved.

First published in 2008 by Melbourne University Press.

Acumen Publishing Limited
4 Saddler Street
Durham
DH1 3NP
www.acumenpublishing.co.uk

ISBN: 978-1-84465-254-9

British Library Cataloguing-in-Publication Data
A catalogue record for this book is available
from the British Library.

Typeset in Warnock Pro.
Printed by Ashford Colour Press Ltd, UK.

Contents

Acknowledgements	vi
1. Manholes and tears	1
2. What a piece of work is a man	14
3. The reins of necessity	45
4. A farewell to arms	63
5. Matisse's hernia	98
6. The private life	129
7. Footnotes to Plato	157
8. Balancing the books	161
Index	173

Acknowledgements

Thanks to Mark Vernon and Steven Gerrard at Acumen for their encouragement. I'm also grateful for the patience and insight of Elisa Berg from MUP. Benython Oldfield from Zeitgeist Media Group deserves thanks for his timely advice.

At the University of Melbourne, thanks to Graham Priest, John Armstrong, Doug Adeney and Len O'Neil for their conversation.

I'm grateful to my friends and family for reading the manuscript. *Vale* Joe Johnson, a keen bookseller and fine friend. Thanks also to David Lebedoff, for his wise counsel, and warm friendship.

To my Nikos and Sophia: thank you for sharing your lounge-room playground with my pens, ink and books. Your curiosity, energy and honesty are a lesson to me. And to Ruth, my amanuensis, first critic and partner in freedom: thank you for it all, my love.

1. Manholes and tears

> I have an aim, which compels me to go on living and for the sake of which I must cope with even the most painful matters. Without this aim I would take things much more lightly – that is, I would stop living.   (Friedrich Nietzsche, letter to Franz Overbeck, Summer 1883)

When my son was a newborn, I often found it easy to soothe his crying. All I had to do was gently tap his back and say *shhh* into his ear. Without fail, he would begin to quieten down. His banshee cries would turn into tiny sobs and eventually he would fall asleep on my shoulder, a little snuggling bundle. At other times, I would sing to him in Arabic scales, with as much depth and vibrato as possible. He would immediately unball his fists, stop crying and stare at me with huge, unblinking blue eyes. The reason for this, I read, was that babies can only give their attention to a couple of things at once. If they are crying, they are crying. If they are listening to their father trying to sound like Nusrat Fateh Ali Khan, then that is their world. In other words, it is almost impossible for them to be in two minds about anything.

As babies get older, these limitations begin to subside. Children become capable of turning their attention to several things at once. Sometimes no amount of midnight singing can stop my toddler from a raging, nightmare-spawned scream. (Poor little fellow – he's listening to *both* of us wailing.) And as his blue eyes have darkened, his mind has become capable of resisting my whims in favour of whims of his own. Like all children, he is learning to see, hear, smell and taste many things at once and to give each sensation and emotion its turn. The upside of this is that he is discovering a whole new world. The downside is that he is very easily distracted: dinner is interrupted by Lego, and Lego by a recycling truck driving past, and so on until bedtime. Of course this will change as he matures. By the time he's older, he will be diversifying his experience of the world while regaining the focused attention of his infancy. Indeed, this is at the heart of growing up: rediscovering our newborn single-mindedness while discovering more things to put our mind to.

Yet the cultivation of concentration can be a struggle. Even as adults, we cannot give our full attention to many things at once. Our perception very quickly becomes divided, patchy and unreliable. Psychologists speak of a "single channel bottleneck": we can perceive only a relatively small amount at once. And even when we *can* broaden our observations, the bottleneck resumes once we try thinking and acting – we get confused, make mistakes, become slower or simply block things out. The upshot is this: whether we like it or not, our perceptions are narrow and our ability to act on them is circumscribed.

Put economically, attention is a scarce and precious resource; frustrating as this might be, we have to be canny with it. When we cannot do this, we're said to be "distracted". The *Oxford English Dictionary* tells us that to distract someone is to "prevent (someone) from giving their full attention to something". For example, while I was writing this book my wife Ruth read the first two paragraphs and immediately wanted to talk about our little boy. In the words of the *Oxford English Dictionary*, she was "preventing her husband from giving his full attention to his book". With her understandable interest in our son, she was distracting me: presenting a stimulus that clogged up my perceptual bottleneck.

But there's more to distraction than a breach of cognitive constraints. Psychological blockages are part of a much larger set of limitations: those of mortal life itself. There are only so many professions, sexual partners, houses, entertainments and amusements available; and we only have so many days to invest in each. To commit to *this* job, *this* spouse, *this* leisure, *this* gadget is to withdraw time, energy and wherewithal from another possibility. This economy extends from the most obvious and pointed life choices to the inestimable, inarticulate decisions we make each and every hour. Put simply, to be human is to be finite – "born to a limited situation", as Goethe put it. Because of this, the good life warrants an ongoing struggle to be clear about what's important, and to seek it with lucidity and passion; not to be distracted by false ambitions, or waylaid by dissipated consciousness. This conundrum is captured in the Latin root of the word *distraction*, meaning literally to tear apart or pull asunder. When we are distracted, we're dragged away from what's worthwhile.

Hence distraction is ultimately a question of value. To say that we're "distracted" is to admit that we're squandering our mental and physical assets; something we value less is diverting our efforts from something we value more (or should). Values represent our choices of what's most significant, desirable or necessary. When we say that something has value, we're really saying: "I have only so much time, and so much energy – *this* is what's best."

But what criteria should we deploy to avoid distraction; what *is* best? A clue lies in the word itself. "Value" comes from the Latin *valere*, meaning "be strong", or "be worthy", and we've kept these meanings in our word "valiant". To be valiant is to be courageous and hardy. However, to the Romans *valere* meant not only to have physical strength but also to have something richer: health and wellbeing. For example, to say *"te valere iubeo"* to a friend was to say "I bid you farewell". All these words – value, valiant, *valere* – stem from a more general idea of strength: being robust, vigorous, vibrant and fecund. This is retained in our current concept of value, even if it's obscured by catchphrases like "economic value" or "family values". To obtain what's valuable is to acquire power, in the finest sense of the word: capacity, capability, energy and enthusiasm. What's valuable is what gives us the potency to cultivate the best life we can within the circumstances we've inherited or created. It enables independence, freedom from coercion and a check against self-deception and delusion. In simple terms, what's valuable is what enhances our liberty.

Importantly, this isn't a liberty of rights and legal privileges – though these can help, of course. And it's not simply being "left alone", as if emancipation were a retreat into selfishness or solipsism. Instead, it's freedom as the development of good character: patiently, passionately crafting oneself, in an imperfect world. This is liberty as existential adventure. What's valuable to me is what encourages, enriches and orients this ambition.

The implications of this are relatively simple but immensely important. At the heart of distraction is not neurophysiology but an ongoing struggle to flourish within the limitations of mortality. We have only one life, and it's marked by all sorts of deprivations, irreversibilities and entrenched habits. And we often have to negotiate these with diminishing hours and flagging potencies. For these reasons, we need to be sincere and judicious in our existential commitments and prudent in our efforts to succeed in each. To be diverted isn't simply to have too many stimuli but to be confused about what to attend to and why. Distraction is the very opposite of emancipation: failing to see what is worthwhile in life, and lacking the wherewithal to seek it.

Of course, we might well disagree about what *are* the most valuable choices for us, but we must make them; there's no asylum from the obligations of existing. What's hopeful in this message is that we needn't waste our precious days – we can be resolute in our embrace of what cultivates liberty and equally firm in our rejection of what leaves us weak, confused or enslaved. In *Twilight of the Idols*, Nietzsche summed up this philosophy with his usual succinctness when he wrote: "Formula of my happiness: a Yes, a No, a straight line, a goal."

The racehorse of genius

Finding the straight line can be difficult, and following it harder still. Distraction can slowly, quietly become part of our identity. A fine example of this comes from Robert Musil's brilliant novel, *The Man Without Qualities*. Set in the Austro-Hungarian Empire just before the First World War, it is an arresting portrait of modern life; of the mechanical, uncanny march to war; of the curious kinship between freedom and paralysis. It also happens to be exceptionally long. Milan Kundera, author of *The Unbearable Lightness of Being*, speaks of *The Man Without Qualities* as one of the two or three books he loves most in the world. Nonetheless, he compares it to "a castle so big it can't be seen all at once" or "a quartet that goes on for nine hours". Musil died before he could finish it, but the final product is a highly intelligent and charming work of literary art. It ranks alongside the novels of Joyce, Proust and Mann as the greatest works of twentieth-century fiction.

The hero is Ulrich, a young Austro-Hungarian who is the epitome of the modern gentleman. He is tall, good-looking, well built and a skilled boxer. He enjoys the fine things in life – food, wine and women – and is capable of manly elegance and refinement. He also happens to be extremely intelligent and very driven. As a young man, Ulrich was convinced that he was destined for glory, and it is clear that he is blessed with the talents to achieve this.

He begins his quest in the cavalry, trying to attain the "lordliness, power and pride" of a general like Napoleon. However, he is soon undone by his fondness for the wives and daughters of civilians, one of whom happens to be friends with the Minister of War. His dreams of world conquest clash with the mess he makes of his romantic dalliances and he is soon out of favour with various senior officers. He quits the military and takes up engineering, which has the boldness of the military along with the new powers of modern technology. The old horses were messy and easily tired, whereas the "new horse had limbs of steel and ran ten times as fast". Yet Ulrich soon discovers that the efficiency and precision of engineering are applied to machines but not to the engineers themselves. They assemble perfectly adapted machines and tools but leave themselves as imperfect as they always were. Ulrich flees engineering and tries his hand at something else, something more perfect and pure: mathematics. Mathematics might seem dull and pedantic, but it is at the heart of all science and therefore of modern life itself. For Ulrich, science is like a magic, "before which God opens one fold of his mantle after another, a religion whose dogma is permeated and sustained by the hard, courageous, mobile, knife-cold, knife-sharp mode of thought that is mathematics". Of course, Ulrich does brilliantly – he becomes a "young man of promise". One day he will be lauded as a sublime genius …

Yet the day never comes. Its impossibility dawns on Ulrich when he reads, in the sports pages of a newspaper, a reference by a journalist to a "racehorse of genius". Not a scientist, a philosopher, or an inventor – a racehorse. In one of those tragically comic epiphanies, Ulrich realizes that this horse, something he used to mount and whip, has beaten him to genius, the "summit of his ambitions". He thought he had left the horses behind when he fled the cavalry, but it seems they left him behind.

Ulrich takes a break from his mathematical research to live the life of a bachelor, complete with a mistress and an expensive apartment. This brings with it a host of diversions and digressions that have little to do with his mathematical achievements. He ends up utterly distracted, listlessly shifting from one thing to another, and unwilling or unable to reclaim the promise of his talent. As author Jane Smiley wrote in the *Guardian*, Ulrich is "going nowhere. He is always right, but never productive, never happy, and never, except momentarily, engaged".

Ulrich is intelligent, motivated and obviously capable of appreciating all manner of fine things – and doing so decisively and prudently. He knows what he values and he is eminently capable of saying yes and no to these goals, just as Nietzsche recommended. He can chase military victory, mathematical clarity and beautiful, love-starved women – these are no problem whatsoever.

Ulrich's problem is that he has never chased the most valuable thing of all: himself. Forever flitting from one project to another, he has never treated himself as a project. Instead, he has fled from mortal doubts and preoccupations into the cooler commonwealth of intellectual or physical competition. Musil writes: "There was something in him that had never wanted to stay anywhere, but has groped its way along the walls of the world, thinking: There are still millions of other walls." Because of this, Ulrich has never cultivated a self – he remains a set of wonderful abilities and accomplishments, without a strong character behind them. Musil writes: "Ulrich had to confess to himself, smiling, that ... he was, after all, a 'character', even without having one." In this sense, Ulrich is not so much a "man without qualities" as a set of qualities without a man. He has lost himself, his project of freedom, to distraction.

In this, Ulrich is emblematic of a more pervasive struggle, a conflict endemic to the human condition. It's what we might call the flight from life, and what the German philosopher Martin Heidegger called "fallenness".

Groundless floating

Heidegger is one of those examples of what I might call "truth with baggage". While he was an unrepentant Nazi sympathizer and sometime philanderer, he was also a brilliant thinker and a penetrating analyst of the human condition. He argued that we spend most of our lives fleeing from our own death. By this, he didn't mean we're over-cautious of buses or fussy with what we eat. What Heidegger meant by "death" was the very finitude that marks our mortality: the limits and constraints we simply cannot avoid.

Of all the captivating possibilities in our lives, death is the one possibility we cannot disavow. And at the same time, it's a mark of authenticity: one of the few genuine possibilities that is ours, and ours alone. No one can die our death on our behalf. If attended seriously, this insight has flow-on effects for life in general: if it is "I" who must die, then it is "I" who must live. If we take up the mantle of existence from birth to expiry, we must accept responsibility for how we live and who to be – and why.

But we often miss this opportunity. As Heidegger suggested, we can easily spend our daily lives avoiding existential responsibility: speaking in clichés and entertaining ourselves with "idle talk". He spoke of *Das Man*, which means "the man" in German but is similar to "they" in English. *Das Man* is the great anonymous public opinion and sentiment, which is everyone in general but no one in particular. For Heidegger, we frequently defer to this anonymous "they" instead of living our own lives. We ease into pleasant or familiar ideas and opinions and never seek confronting reality – Heidegger also called it a "groundless floating".

Seen through Heidegger's gaze, Ulrich's diversions make sense – but so do ours. Distractions – from trashy supermarket magazines, to shallow relationships, to jobs we loathe but flee to – are often our way to elude the existential burden: deciding what we are and what to be. There's something essentially human in all this. As T. S. Eliot wrote in his poem "Burnt Norton", "human kind cannot bear very much reality". While we might not be fleeing mortality, we often distract ourselves from pain, heartache or boredom.

An age of distractions

It can be genuinely consoling to admit that we all struggle to seize life's elusive potential. With a combination of *Schadenfreude* and relief, I certainly feel much better when I read of Karl Marx's chaotic work habits. A Prussian spy who observed Marx's house in Soho wrote of his "topsy-turvy" front-room, with "several cups with broken rims ... an inkpot, tumblers, Dutch clay pipes, tobacco ash" strewn everywhere. Marx apparently found all his domestic arrangements difficult, and spoke of producing "miniature dunghills" after his daughter Eleanor was born. When he did get the time to work on what he once called his "economic shit", he would embroil himself in petty disputes with lesser scholars, even challenging mortified writers and editors to duels. (And I thought my hours spent watching *Doctor Who* were wasteful.)

However, the modern age affords more opportunities for distraction than Marx could have imagined. Most obviously, there is the ubiquity of noise (from the Latin *nausea*), which amply demonstrates the strain on our attention. Recent studies suggest that long-term exposure to noise leads to some 200,000 deaths per year. Aural pollution, from sources ranging from pubs and clubs to traffic, is quite literally giving people heart attacks.

But there are more subtle, more chronic problems with noise. For example, a Cornell University study concluded that children from schools under aeroplane flight paths have more difficulty learning language. As they adapt to the noise of the jet engines, they "filter out" the human voice and its expressive nuances. The din doesn't simply silence us – it can deprive us of our capacity to speak and be heard.

And these industrial distractions are accompanied by those of advertising and leisure. Music blares in lifts, malls and train stations, and cafés and bars have wall-sized televisions. In these circumstances, intimate conversation is hampered, along with quiet reflection. If this cacophony doesn't directly fracture our consciousness, it hampers our efforts to determine what will – to clearly and decisively seek what's valuable.

Pervasive as it is, ambient noise is not the only distraction. For many of us, the site of the most frustrating diversions and interruptions is work. In numerous organizations, for example, employees are "on call" well beyond office hours. In the service of promotion and profit, time with intimates or one's own counsel is surrendered. And perhaps more pressingly, there is an impression that these sacrifices are necessary and laudable: that good workers are *always* available and good bosses can guiltlessly avail themselves of this resource. The result can be an inability to properly perceive, think and imagine; a dissolution of consciousness, which affects health, peace of mind, and close relationships. Scholars from Rutgers University have recently predicted a spate of litigations as workers sue their bosses for the "detrimental outcomes" of office technology: addiction, stress, exhaustion. Perhaps the first litigant will be someone like Candace Falk, whose husband brings his handheld computer to bed every night. "It's a kind of ménage à trois that I didn't choose," Candace told a *New York Times* reporter, "but there it is, every day and night." This incursion of employment into after-hours life is distraction on the march: the slow, sometimes unnoticed disappearance of free time, unaccounted-for attention.

But most striking are the distractions we enthusiastically choose: those of fun and leisure, not those of workaday responsibility. Whether it's digital entertainment or the fickle world of online friendship, we often *seek* distraction. We chase the noise of the iPod, the simple resolution of the Hollywood blockbuster or the false spontaneity of online browsing. This isn't forced upon us by class, status, geography or dumb luck – we heartily, eagerly embrace it.

And one reason for this urge is Heidegger's "fallenness": the preoccupation affords a reprieve from the anxieties of life, which confront us in moments of repose. "We are afraid that when we are alone and quiet," wrote Nietzsche, Heidegger's philosophical progenitor, "something will be whispered into our ear." This "something" is our own conscience and awareness; the lingering, nagging realization that there are realities to be confronted, choices to be made; the knowledge that opportunities are diminishing with our days. If there is an internet terminal or pulp film handy, the so-called "call of conscience" is easily silenced or suppressed.

Of course, we should by wary of slandering our age: distraction is *not* a purely modern malaise. Given Heidegger's observations about the human condition, the tendency to flee our private demons is an ancient one. History is replete with examples of amusements, entertainments and cheap diversions. English diarist Samuel Pepys witnessed the public hanging and mutilation of a Puritan soldier in 1660. As if he were describing a ticker-tape parade for athletes, he wrote of the poor man, "cut down, and his head and heart shown to the people", who greeted his organs with "great shouts of joy". There's nothing like "shock and awe" to occupy a weary mind, as the producers of our latest wars know all too well. But our distractions need not be violent or cruel – benign gossip or addictive games will do just as well. The compulsion to seek respite is as ancient as humanity itself, and it stems from our understandable unwillingness to look our own lives squarely in the face.

Any critique of modern life must therefore be a nuanced one. Our digital age certainly affords opportunities for distraction – in its acceleration, interconnection and relentlessness, it can be overwhelming. As I argue in another chapter, if we are careless or thoughtless, technology can be the perfect, addictive distraction. And in today's politics, art, work and relationships, there are opportunities for divided, diminished consciousness; for the squandering of valuable insights and intimacies. But this doesn't mean we're slaves to mechanical innovation or instantaneous entertainment. We cannot blame technology for our own flights, inattention or willingness to be falsely consoled. And distraction doesn't warrant paranoia or recrimination – it's not a doomsday proclamation, where we *must* succumb. Instead, the contemporary glut of diversions is an opportunity for reflection. Despite our best intentions, distractions can blunt our mental keenness and make the flight from existence more convenient, if not more palatable.

And this convenience is at the heart of distraction – not simply that we're assailed by unrewarding stimuli, but that we seek them or learn to enjoy them. "How we labour at our daily work more ardently and thoughtlessly than is necessary to sustain our life," wrote Nietzsche in his *Untimely Meditations*, "because it is even more necessary not to have leisure to stop and think. Haste is universal because everyone is in flight from himself." If we lament the speed and fracturing of life, we can also welcome these as a refuge from the burden of the self; from the responsibility to live. In this state, it's difficult to identify what's valuable, and almost impossible to seek it with lucidity and determination. The result is diminished opportunity for liberty.

The indignity of manholes

Woody Allen, in his comedy *Bananas*, offered an elegant metaphor for distraction. Allen plays Fielding Mellish, a clumsy schmuck who cannot seem to think of anyone but himself – Allen's usual shtick. But ironically, his "self" is brilliantly, hilariously pathetic. He hates his job, is psychologically oppressed by his parents and seems unable to connect emotionally with women. In one scene, Fielding is in a car, trying to impress a pretty girl with his self-righteous philosophizing. In his whiny New York patois, he says to her: "To a guy like me, the greatest crimes are the crimes against human dignity." He then steps out of the car and falls down a manhole.

In a moment of perfect putzery, Woody Allen summed up distraction concisely. It's not difficult to be so engrossed that we fail to notice threats to our wellbeing, like a gaping hole in the ground. There's something enduringly human about his hapless, bumbling lack of foresight. But Fielding's accident is also a motif for his life as a whole. He is fundamentally short-sighted: about who and what he values in life, and why. Vacillating between hedonism and fear, dissimulation and tactless sincerity, he stumbles from one farce to another. By the middle of the film, he's the unwilling leader of a Latin American revolutionary army, chafing at privation and danger. "Freedom is wonderful," he says to the revolutionaries. "On the other hand, if you're dead, it's a drawback to your sex life." At the heart of Mellish's native hilarity is an inability to commit to the project of himself; to a life worth living, or dying for.

Mellish is the endemic, human-all-too-human face of distraction. If it flourishes in the digital age, it has always existed. It is the failing of a finite existence. The most rewarding response to this is neither a return to some mythical "simpler time" nor a withdrawal to privative fantasy. It's not glib satisfaction with the status quo, or frenzied revolution (and certainly not with Mellish as our *commandante*). Instead, a life without distraction demands an exploration: of the enrolment and exhaustion of our capacities and of their relationship to what's valuable in life. We have to interrogate and illuminate the ways in which our attention is exploited and coerced, and to assess how it might be differently engaged. We have to examine not simply what we put our minds to but what we put our lives to.

To this end, *Distraction* looks into the lives of artists, scholars and statesmen, whose struggles have helped to clarify my own. From Spinoza's lens grinding, to Heidegger's artistic blinkers, to Henry James's amorous epiphanies, their successes and failures put my own into perspective. They illuminate or inspire my pursuit of what's worthwhile in life. The prize is the very thing poor Fielding Mellish was clumsily fighting for: freedom.

2. What a piece of work is a man

The feeling of being fit to work again does much for a man. Unfortunately, I am constantly interrupted by social troubles and lose a lot of time. Thus, for example, the butcher has suspended meat supplies today, and by Saturday even my stock of paper will be used up.

(Karl Marx, letter to Friedrich Engels, 7 August 1866)

Karl Marx was a curious mix of idler and workaholic. As we've seen, he was often distracted from his important work by petty disputes, domestic chaos and illness. If the portly, scruffy philosopher wasn't fidgeting or pacing, his fiery temperament led him astray. And when *A Contribution to a Critique of Political Economy* didn't live up to Marx's hype, his easily diverted character was to blame: despite all his self-congratulation, he simply hadn't put the work in. "Alas," said his friend Engels, "we are so used to these excuses for the non-completion of work!" Admittedly, it's hard to concentrate on the revolution when your arse boils are flaring up ("of all types of work," said Marx in a letter to Engels, "theory is the most unsuitable if one has this devil's brew in one's blood"). Yet Marx's chaotic home, unpaid bills and life of impetuous feuds give the impression of a disorganized teenager in a man's shaggy body.

But appearances can be deceptive. Marx was a prodigious writer, speaker and teacher, as well as an international organizer for the communist cause. Perhaps he fell short of his own aspirations, but this is merely testament to their loftiness, rather than to his laziness.

Pushing him to burn the midnight oil despite his proclivities was a deep-seated desire to make himself heard. More crucially, he wished to see his ideas come alive in broader society – to persuade, bully, mock and inspire with his works. This fervent pragmatism was captured in his well-known (perhaps infamous) slogan from *Theses on Feuerbach*: "The philosophers have only interpreted the world, in various ways; the point is to change it." If anything was work, this was it (even if it didn't mean overalls and a punch card).

Marx's reputation makes it easy to forget this. He is known as a fierce critic of capitalist society, lambasting its cruelty to workers – the phrase "alienation of labour" is an incantation of sorts. But what this veils is Marx's own commitment to work as well as his philosophical celebration of it. In many ways, Marx wasn't simply a detractor of work – he was a utopian defender of its singular virtues. This very optimistic attitude to work, rather than being contradictory, was affirmed by a systematic and often profound philosophy (which he would later call a "science"). It saw work not simply as a dreary biological or economic duty but as the very thing that raised us above the brutes.

The ideal of work

In *Economic and Philosophical Manuscripts of 1844* (written by Marx when he was only twenty-six), the philosopher set out an ambitious theory of man, work and the environment – workers could be understood not as isolated individuals (billiard balls with pay cheques) but as creative creatures intimately related to the environment. And Marx was speaking not of the man-made environment but of nature – what he called man's "inorganic body". By this, he meant that we are part of the natural environment, and all our achievements are supported or limited by the resources of the earth. Even if we're desk jockeys or check-out chicks, we're still utilizing and distributing the goods of the planet (from junk food to gold in computers). Marx's point was that no job, however high tech, is ethereal – it might seem very abstract or informational, but we're always working in a tangle of real, physical, tangible stuff. And this is what keeps us going – we eat, shit, sweat and breathe, and none of this is negotiable. Regardless of how minutely we can print on a silicon chip, we're bound by all sorts of natural laws. To live, we have to destroy, transform and create, just like animals – this is the basis of all work.

What raises us humans above other species, for Marx, is that we're *free* to work, and to work creatively. We don't just work when we have to; we construct, write and cook out of curiosity and ambition and for fun. As Marx put it, "an animal only produces what it immediately needs for itself or its young ... whilst man produces even when he is free from physical need." More importantly, we love to surround ourselves by the things we create: clothes, houses, foods, books, films, trinkets. And in doing so, we're not just feeding our bodies or seeking procreation – we're confronting ourselves in our own artefacts, whether those crafted from wood and steel or the virtual "stuff" of magnetically recorded ones and zeros. We encounter our unique humanity in objects to be examined, shaped and appreciated. This is crucial for the health and flourishing of our psyche, because we reflect on our own condition. "Man makes his life," wrote Marx, "actively itself the object of his will and of his consciousness." Put another way, work is worthwhile when it enables sustained and sensitive attention to life. It isn't just a battle with the weather or predators – it's a way to mould and shape our own nature. This is why Marx called creative labour our "species being" – it is how homo sapiens fashions itself.

Of course, there is more to enjoyable work than Marx's philosophy immediately suggests. Even when it's menial donkey work, employment can have a host of other pay-offs. It allows workers to socialize, to collaborate and to gain recognition or status.

Sometimes we don't want a raise – we just want a pat on the back or a "thank you" (even if it's in an email). At other times, work allows a welcome break from the unheralded drudgery of domestic labour – the sweeping, washing, cooking and scrubbing (not to mention the burlesque farce that is shit-filled nappies). Many mothers need work not just for cash but for sanity, to spend a little time with grown-ups who can string sentences together and empathize about the struggles of adulthood or parenthood. Work is a social enterprise, and we are – as Aristotle stressed – social animals. But at the end of the day, the crucial criterion for rewarding work is the work itself. If work doesn't allow us to see a little of ourselves alive in the world (and hopefully the best of ourselves), then it all seems pointless.

Marx was resentful of interruptions and the demands of industry, for these very reasons. In his writing, he was cultivating himself and his audiences by supplying articulate reflections on life. Instead of being consumed by the abject struggle with want, he was leaving a little of himself behind (perhaps the finest part). Marx was doing precisely what he endorsed: "he duplicated himself not only ... intellectually, but also actively, in reality, and ... contemplates himself in a world he has created." The significance of this is that it removes ambiguity and mysticism from Marx's recalcitrance. It reveals that his peculiar combination of diligence and indolence was the mark of someone who knew the precious, personal value of work: as the extension and cultivation of humanity.

As we've seen, Marx wouldn't have suggested *all* work was this edifying. To begin, much of our labour is still a struggle to get by. Even if Marx had his maids and cooks – he was, after all, a gentleman – he still recognized the unshakable bond between work and need. We need to eat, to wash, to find shelter, and these things aren't provided gratis by Mother Earth. And after the needs of nature come the demands of men. As Marx was keen to point out, most work is simply the replacement of one necessity with another: the laws of the economy become as commonsensical as those of metabolism and circulation. Even if we don't catch or cook our own fish (Marx's favourite dish), we still have to pay the bills (or, in Marx's case, get Engels to pay them). The lesson is simple: even if you're bankrolled by the son of a wealthy industrialist, necessity will out. In the economy, as in the jungle, there's often no such thing as a free lunch.

But the Marxist theory of labour is not without baggage. In Marx's work, there's a real tension between the ideal of creative labour and the means to realize it in our lives. For Marx, creative labour could only flourish in a socialist society, where the workers' citizenry owns and runs industry (as well as government). It's a genuine democratic communist nation, rather than an oligarchy of the bourgeoisie. But this ideal nation is at odds with life as we know it. As Marx saw it, the bourgeoisie have a stake in the status quo, which they'll maintain with violence and coercion (contemporary pundits would point to America's interference in socialist Cuba and Venezuela as examples). Basically, this means that creative labour can't create the conditions for its own existence.

At this point, Marx offers two different but related suggestions. First, the workers must overthrow capitalist States, seize the equipment of governance and production, and put down reactionaries – the so-called "dictatorship of the proletariat". Secondly, Marx implies that this *will* happen eventually, since history is moving logically according to dialectical laws. In his terms (borrowed from Hegel), the "contradictions of capitalism" would work themselves out, with communism as the end result (Engels spoke of the "inevitable downfall" of capitalism). It offers a utopia of labour, which is either the inevitable destiny of mankind (so it's best to just wait), or the bittersweet fruit of glorious thuggery (so it's best to savage each other).

For employees sitting in cubicles or assembly lines, this gospel can be, ironically, profoundly alienating. They find themselves either waiting helplessly for the tide of history to turn – maybe tomorrow, in a few years, in a century – or faced with a terrible responsibility: murdering their fellow citizens or destroying their country in internecine violence. In this light, creative labour seems an airy phantom for tomorrow's lucky inheritors, or a bloodstained prize for today's brutal malcontents (who can use the "inevitability" of history as a gloss on their brutality). But it leaves most with a wonderful vision of collaboration and creativity, without the means to achieve this in a civilized way.

Still, in Marx's stubborn working habits, and his ideals of creative labour, we retain a glimpse of the worth of work here and now, and how individuals might redeem it. If anything, it's a gentle reminder of priorities: behind his lapsed bills, messy home and grumpy demeanour was a genuine belief in the nobility and necessity of work. This demonstrates the vital difference he identified: between labour at its most menial and work at its most edifying. If we do spend so much of our life chasing security and physiological contentment, the ambition that drives our work is crucial. For Marx, work needn't be thoughtless, impersonal drudgery. It can improve our potencies and give us a richer and more vivid picture of ourselves. We needn't shirk elbow grease or paper shuffling, but nor should we be ashamed of our longing to be more human and the belief that work should service this aspiration. In short, work can be fulfilling, creative, enriching – a means to cultivate our character.

The crucible of work

Yet, it'd be foolish to always expect this level of fulfilment from professional life. Today, much of our working life seems to oscillate between profound satisfaction and abhorrent drudgery. But between these two extremes are a wealth of other motivations and rewards. We're pushed to work by all sorts of anxieties and fears, which often have very little to do with paying the bills or transcending our present humanity. We might feel guilty about not living up to parents' expectations, or desperate for peer recognition. If we're parents, we might simply want to escape the claustrophobic confines of home for the peace and quiet of the office. Work can offer us a place to transform these passions into something constructive. And in this, it offers more achievable benefits, alongside Marx's ambitious outlook. Even in banal or boring work, we find a way to make our wayward proclivities productive.

A classic example of the usefulness of work is the poet and critic T. S. Eliot. He once wrote that an artist must lead a "commonplace life" if he's to get any work done. At first blush, it might seem that Thomas Sterns Eliot was the very model of commonplace domesticity and professionalism. In fact, a précis of his life paints him as a bit boring. He married young, cared deeply for his family and was a committed Christian. At parties and social functions he was often dull and forgettable or seemed shy or aloof ("he seemed rather ordinary," said one old schoolmate). To many he appeared a very run-of-the-mill, stuffy, reserved civil servant – perhaps the cartoonish stereotype of a Lloyds bank employee, which indeed he was for almost a decade. Aldous Huxley spoke of him as "the most bank-clerky of all bank clerks". Of his public persona, the lines from his own *Love Song of J. Alfred Prufrock* seem to fit: "an easy tool, / Deferential, glad to be of use, / Politic, cautious, and meticulous; /... a bit obtuse". Quite commonplace indeed.

Yet Eliot's life – private and literary – was quite extraordinary. To begin, his marriage was exceptionally bad. His wife Vivien was vivacious, intelligent and loyal (in her way) and was genuinely interested in enlivening Eliot's life and career. But she was also weak physically and mentally ("a frail creature", according to Herbert Read). Often very ill, Mrs Eliot spent months bedridden and weeks abroad for "cures". She was also sensitive, and increasingly paranoid, qualities that made their marriage unbearable in the end. She accused Eliot of having numerous affairs, while she herself slept with the famous philosopher Bertrand Russell (known to many as "Dirty Bertie"). It's genuinely painful reading Eliot's grateful letters to Russell: "Vivien says you have been quite the angel to her," he wrote in one, seemingly unaware of their affair. As Eliot himself was sometimes shy to the point of misanthropy, prone to cold detachment and sexually dysfunctional (he suffered what he called "nervous sexual attacks" in Paris and London), their two temperaments led to an increasingly fraught marriage. For years Eliot ministered attentively to his wife, but then he slowly grew withdrawn. Increasingly bitter, Vivien mocked and taunted him in company, desperate for some kind of emotional intimacy, even if this were anger or loathing. The inevitable outcome was illness – they made each other sick, quite literally.

During this turmoil, and to pay for Vivien's drugs and treatments, Eliot took a job as a schoolteacher ("for which he is too good," wrote Vivien) but he was eventually offered a post at Lloyds bank. He worked there for almost a decade. As Vivien needed peace and quiet, she sometimes took a cottage in the countryside, where she and her husband would rest on weekends. Eliot would commute to London during the week, rising two hours earlier to work on his philosophy and poetry. While his wife convalesced, Eliot was working furiously, keeping up the habits of a banking clerk while also pursuing a career as a writer, reviewer and part-time lecturer. "I have been busier than most men are in a lifetime," he told an editor. After an unavoidable breakdown (he was often bedridden with lung ailments), Eliot was forced to take three months off work to rest and recuperate. But it didn't last. As soon as he was well, he threw himself back into the grind. His friends were worried that Lloyds was wasting his hours and spoiling his talent (a Cambridge don found him in his dingy office, "stooping, very like a dark bird in a feeder"). And indeed, Eliot's own list of his duties was truly menial, like tabulating the profits of foreign banks. But Eliot said he enjoyed it – it gave him regularity and order, and it assuaged his guilt at leading the life of a poet, instead of a minister of religion or a businessman.

The private motivations that pushed Eliot into his gruelling professional regime – poverty and illness – provided a powerful urgency: Vivien's health couldn't be let to degenerate. But added to the pressures of economy and physiology were the curious drives of Eliot's psyche. Eliot was born in St Louis, to a traditional Unitarian home. Popular in New England (where the Eliots were a well-known family), the Unitarian church pushed traditional Protestant values: austerity, hard work, restraint and social welfare. "Make the best of every faculty," wrote his mother to her children, "and control every tendency to evil." Like many American Protestants, Eliot grew up in a household where good Christians were expected to live a respectable public life, independent and upright. And added to this were his mother's personal hopes. Deprived of an opportunity to attend college, the very bright and driven Charlotte Eliot wanted her son to succeed – "I hope in your literary work," she wrote to her son, "you will receive early the recognition I strove for and failed."

Eliot repudiated his Unitarian upbringing (he was baptised an Anglican in 1927, aged thirty-nine), but the pressure to work stayed with him. He was agonized by his decision to leave America, give up academic security and embrace the literary life of London. "You are so good and kind with offers of help," he wrote to his mother from England, "I should like to work day and night without stopping just to make up for it." When his father died in 1919, Eliot was crushed, knowing the old man went to the grave thinking his son an idle and foolish failure. Whether it was inhuman hours at the bank, or volunteering as a fire warden during World War II, Eliot was trying to overcome his very Unitarian sense of uselessness.

Eliot's Christianity also suggests another strong motivation for work. When he spoke of his need for regular habits, he was expressing a deeper yearning for order in the world. For him, most of life was mere "play" – a meaningless tangle of semblance and illusion, with no apparent meaning; and, behind the appearance of everyday chaos, nothing – at least nothing rational (what he called "the void"). He yearned for God to fill this abyss but only found Him in glimpses. At the root of his religious life was a deep and enduring uncertainty. For Eliot, a steady, difficult and demanding job was an earthly incarnation of God's plan – it brought discipline and clarity to the world. It kept insanity at bay and took his mind off threats and anxieties. Undoubtedly, the banal but rigorous duties of banking and lecturing were attractive alternatives to his wife's suffering and to his own spiritual pathos. For most of his adult life, Eliot sought restraint, order and discipline in adopted Englishness ("too correct," said Herbert Read), religion and poetry ("there is only good verse, bad verse, and chaos"). But he also found it in Lloyds bank, and in the offices of publishing house Faber and Faber.

The overall impression of Eliot is of a man of great intellectual and emotional intensity, beset by equally potent anxieties and prejudices; a man very much like his Prufrock, "sprawling as a pin". He saw sex as an "evil" (but not boring, like the "cheery automatism" of so many moderns) and was threatened by women's sexuality and physiology. He was terrified of public shame or embarrassment, but made his life as a writer. He was scared of cows. He could sometimes be lively and charming ("the soul of gaiety," said literary scholar Bonamy Dobrée), and his youthful letters to Conrad Aiken contained charming drawings, jokes and ribaldry (English seamen to German sailors: "What ho! they cry'd, we'll sink your ship! / And so they up and sink'd her. / But the cabin boy was sav'd alive / And bugger'd, in the sphincter"). But his intense reserve, uncertainty and aloof manner were what many noticed, particularly as he grew older. For most of his married life with Vivien (he remarried happily as an older man), he was frustrated and resentful, and his friendships were often riddled with enmity or mistrust. Confronted by this uncertainty and perceived hostility, Eliot threw himself into work. What was ushered in by abject want was fired by a deep-seated longing for usefulness and regularity.

And the hard work paid off. As a writer he became the embodiment of modern poetry for a generation and received the highest international honours and awards (including the Nobel Prize for Literature). As an editor he published some of the world's best writers. His self-confessed "dependence on work" tortured him, but it left one of the finest literary legacies in modern history ("READ HIM," ordered Ezra Pound in a poem for his late friend).

Eliot's combination of industry, nervous energy and faith isn't as idiosyncratic as it might appear. In *The Protestant Ethic and the Spirit of Capitalism*, German sociologist Max Weber gave a brilliant account of the curious relationship between religion, psychology and capitalism. Published at the beginning of the twentieth century, in the epoch of modern industrial growth, Weber revealed the very Christian urges behind hard work and money-making.

It might seem absurd to see pecuniary acquisition and Christianity as bedfellows – after all, it was Christ who assaulted the money-lenders in the temple, while generations of Catholic monks renounced property and cash for contemplation in the cloisters. But in modern Protestantism Weber found an intense and sustained industry, which pushed good Christians into profit-making or labour and which lived on in the lives of moderns like Eliot.

At the heart of Protestantism was what we might call an "aristocracy of salvation". For the Calvinists, the world was neatly divided up into the elect, who were given eternal life with God, and the damned. God knew who was who, and Christians could do absolutely nothing about it. No confession, absolution, dispensation, indulgence or magical prayer could save the Hell-bound Puritan. And no amount of love for neighbours or family made any difference either – each was alone with his faith and sin, and his fate was written by God long before his birth. This was a Heavenly Kingdom of very isolated, lonely, helpless sheep, far away from their divine shepherd. Weber argued that, while other Protestant churches (like Pietists in Germany, and Methodists and Baptists in Britain and the United States) departed from his philosophy, they were still citizens in the grand aristocratic state of God: you were either with Him or against Him, God's decision was final, and no correspondence would be entered into.

At first glance, the Protestant universe might seem like a thoroughly depressing vision of spirituality – hardly the breeding ground for generations of diligent Eliots. And for many it was a profoundly paralysing, mortifying world. But precisely because of this threat, Protestantism led to a heightened interest in labour and a bafflingly good conscience about pecuniary gain.

Not knowing whether they were doomed to the Inferno or promised paradise, the Protestants had no alternative other than to demonstrate their faith: God *had* given them His grace, they *were* one of the elect, and Eternal Glory was theirs. But this could not be achieved by sitting about in monastic cells or scurrying up a mountain for starvation and enlightenment. To show themselves and fellow Puritans their fidelity to the Lord, Protestants had to provide evidence, as it were. And this evidence was work. The idea wasn't to enjoy some mystical unity with God but to be God's instrument on earth. This couldn't be slap-dash or piecemeal, because the slightest slip-up might betray a damned soul. Life as an efficient tool of Jehovah meant no idleness, laziness, sloth.

For Weber, this was the perfect psychological mechanism for the good capitalist and his workers. It led the penitent sinner to plan their life in a meticulous and painstaking way, seizing any and all opportunities to glorify God and prove their good soul. Without succour from friends or family, it made them more individualistic and hard-minded, and less likely to be relaxed and easy going. Weber's point was that, while all civilizations have greed and an appetite for money, this so-called "ascetic Protestantism" led to a unique modern achievement: the rational, rigorous worker, loving fortitude, fearing uselessness and boredom, and hating indolence. Work supplied Calvinists and their kin with a balm against crushing self-doubt while at the same time giving their lives order and regularity. And because they disliked ostentation and excess, they grew rich – thrift combined with diligence to produce mountains of profit (when he died in 1965, Eliot left an estate worth over £100,000). For Weber, sober Christian zeal was the spirit of capitalism.

As T. S. Eliot's earnest working life suggests, the effects of this approach continued well after the West killed God (or let him die, to use a contemporary bioethics distinction). And in Eliot we see many of the themes of Weber's sociological analysis. His loneliness, self-sufficiency, thrift, diligence and desire for rational order – all of these traits belong to the Puritan, which of course Eliot was in many ways. While his childhood Unitarianism lacked the metaphysical rumination of Calvinism (let alone Catholicism), this no-nonsense attitude was itself classically Puritan: those invigorated with the spirit of the Lord don't have time for navel gazing. Some might see poetry as time-wasting, but for Eliot it was a vocation – a "calling", in Luther's sense of the word. Of course, Eliot was quite critical of his boyhood Puritanism. He saw it as hollow, robbed of the profound and enduring significance of the Catholic mysteries. His *Athenaeum* portrait of the Boston writer Henry Adams described the Unitarian as "seeking education, with the wings of a beautiful but ineffectual conscience, beating vainly in a vacuum jar". For Eliot, this disoriented flight was the product of Christianity without mystical commitments – it foundered in its own modern liberalism. But born and raised a New England Protestant (even in Missouri), Eliot couldn't shrug off the habits of a lifetime. As a faithful, guilty worker, he exemplified Weber's thesis – not for naught did the young poet Robert Lowell call Eliot "a tireless Calvinist".

But Weber's point was that the Protestant ethic went beyond Christians; the character of modern capitalism is profoundly shaped by their ascetic habits. This is significant, because it suggests that there is a large middle-ground of anxiety, peer recognition and longing between the utopian urges of Marx's creative labour and the basic struggle with want. Today atheists and Christians alike are often driven to work by a host of "Protestant" desires and terrors. For some, it is guilt – a debt owed to family, or the abstract goods of State or the "taxpayers". For others, it's a need to overcome loneliness or boredom, or to rise above what was once called the mass of idle sinners (nowadays called the "unemployed"). For others still, it's a fervent desire for order and meaning, making the chaos of the psyche, or home life, tolerable. Like Eliot, many spouses today flee domesticity to the workplace, where hard work is praised and there's no endless nagging from partners or kids. They are seeking precisely what Eliot sought: order, usefulness, and a break from chaos at home (or in their own heads). If church attendance is waning, the Protestant ethic is alive and well in every worker seeking solace and salvation in ungodly hours.

The implication of Eliot's success is that, with sufficient presence of mind, we can use work as it uses us. While it takes our hours and energies, it also serves as a redemption for many of our idiosyncrasies and proclivities. Even if we're drawn to work because of loneliness, guilt or a longing for respect, it can provide a site for the commitment of the unruly psyche to something constructive. While God might be well and truly absent from our labours, work can offer a salvation of sorts: it's a crucible in which our passions are transformed into tangible rewards. Despite its often abject motivations, it offers the realization and intensification of our potencies. In this sense, work is not a distraction from our finest aspirations but a way of strengthening and deepening our capacity to achieve them – it's training for what we *really* want to do in life.

Time and money

Marx and Eliot exemplify work at its most ennobling, if not its most enjoyable. Even if employment is boring, banal and exhausting, it can take us much closer to what we really want out of life. It can sharpen our skills, offer us camaraderie and discipline, and give us opportunities to gain a more lucid view of ourselves. Both Eliot and Marx, despite their resentment of drudgery, spent their lives on the job – and their efforts were rewarded with impressive achievements, genuine recognition, and no small amount of personal pride.

But there's a fine line between workmanlike persistence and abject exploitation. Drive and persistence can easily be misguided, waylaid, perverted – in a word, distracted, from more rewarding aims. This is particularly so in the context of business, where the profit motive easily usurps that of creative labour – it's no coincidence that both urges are captured in the word *industry*. What begins as a sincere exhortation to work more responsibly and seriously becomes an unwitting invitation to mental lethargy and physical exhaustion. The greatest champions of labour can mistakenly be the gaolers of their fellow citizens. And in the process, employment loses its capacity to transform our inclinations and proclivities into constructive, creative labour (as it did for Eliot).

As Eliot's nervous breakdowns and enduring misery imply, these urges can readily lead to the grossest exploitation. The employees who pride themselves on their productivity and punctuality are also the most profitable. The race to be "employee of the month" usually pays more dividends for bosses and shareholders than it does for earnest professional Puritans. And as Weber noted, all sorts of suffering and inequality seem reasonable in a "spiritual aristocracy": the poverty and misery of so many workers living hand to mouth isn't unfair – it's because they don't work hard enough or possess "entrepreneurial spirit". The same pyramid of accomplishment celebrates the wealth and status of the "winners".

They might be exhausted, unhealthy and lonely, but this is the price of salvation.

Take the American scholar and statesman Benjamin Franklin, whom Weber cited as the "spirit of capitalism". Franklin believed wholeheartedly in hard work, even from a young age. As a boy in Boston, he was apprenticed to his brother James at a printery. A few years later, James founded an independent newspaper, the *New England Courant*. Not too long after, Benjamin was submitting his own articles under a pseudonym ("Mrs. Silence Dogood") so that his family wouldn't stop him. After a falling-out with his family, he fled to Philadelphia (with a quick sojourn in London), where he made his name. We might expect the son of a candle-maker to have humble ambitions, but Franklin was unstoppable. He conducted research on electricity, inventing the lightning rod, and developed a catheter, a stove and bifocals (in the spirit of the common good, he patented none of them). He founded a public library, a tertiary college and a hospital and, as ambassador to France, the United States' ally, was crucial in the US victory over Britain. He was also the most important American writer of his generation, his intelligent prose and firm morality capturing the fledgling American imagination. Franklin wasn't just a brilliant polymath – he was diligence embodied.

In addition to being a statesman, a physicist, an engineer, an inventor and a moralist, Franklin was also something of an economist. In his earnest but patronizing "Advice to a Young Tradesman", Franklin argued that idleness and amusement were wastes of money. A man who works only part-time, then spends his cash on theatres or travel, is throwing away his income – twice: once by spending it, and again by stopping work. "Time is money," wrote Franklin famously; every squandered minute is forgone wealth.

In his 1729 pamphlet "A Modest Enquiry into the Nature and Necessity of Paper Currency", Franklin dug a little deeper. Time is money because it measures our work. An hour's work is an hour's work, regardless of what's being provided or produced. To allow us to exchange goods and services, we give this time a price, usually per hour. We can then swap an hour's agriculture for an hour's accounting, without having to worry about the relative values of milking cows and crunching numbers – money makes all labour equal. In this sense, national and international markets are nothing more than the buying and selling of labour. In Franklin's words, "the riches of a country are to be valued by the quantity of labour its inhabitants are able to purchase." This quantity of labour is time – hours, days, minutes. Countries, companies and bosses gain wealth by buying as much of this time as possible – the more time, the more money (for them, at least).

But in order to do this, time itself has to be standardized. To calculate a profitable exchange of money, we need uniform time-keeping. We need to be able to determine how many minutes were worked, and to try to cram as much labour as possible into these minutes. For Franklin, every tick of the clock was another shilling.

It wasn't always so. For most of the world until the Industrial Revolution, time was vaguer. A day was dawn, noon and sundown. Dates were wedded to seasons or lunar cycles, and every town and city was the centre of a new temporal order. Rather than "time", there were "times". With the invention of clockwork devices, and advances in communication and transport, countries were able to develop a consistent time, measurable to fractions of a second. This allowed corporations and bosses to control investment and profit more tightly. One hundred years ago, Nietzsche was already feeling anxious and restless as the reins of the clock grew ever tighter. "One thinks with a watch in one's hand," he wrote in 1887, "even as one eats one's midday meal while reading the latest news of the stock-market." By the early twentieth century, so-called "time and motion" men were barging into factories to accelerate production. Even in the 1960s, they were streamlining the production line, speeding up the clocks, and blacking out the windows (just in case the daylight or a view interfered with clock time).

Nowadays, our time-keeping is even more meticulous. Forget the hour, minute and second – even the nanosecond is passé. We now have the ludicrously short femtosecond. "In a femtosecond," writes James Gleick in *Faster*, "the Concorde flies less than the width of an atom." The more precisely we can measure time, the more efficiently we can manipulate the world, and one another.

Modern business knows the importance of precision in time-keeping. We read constantly about the "cost of X for business", where "X" is time lost to talking, thinking, going to the toilet, eating, or all of the above. Workplace bullying in America apparently costs over a hundred million dollars every year, and work-related depression tens of billions. In 2005 the website Salary.com reported that American "employers spend $759 billion per year on salaries for which real work was expected, but not actually performed." It seems that every drop of time spilled is a dollar down the drain. Today's corporate world has taken Franklin's motto to heart: time is money – and businesses want both, in precise quantities.

Busywork

But Franklin would have been aghast at the consequences of this. The trouble with the accelerated workplace isn't lack of profit. The problem is that it's often impossible to get any work done – what is supposed to be cutting-edge employment turns out to be busywork. Mind-boggling amounts of information are instantly available, everywhere across the "wired" (and increasingly wireless) planet. This isn't just useful data, it's also pointless news, group emails, spam, viruses, irrelevant corporate memos, joke forwards, and so on. Each one of these is a distraction. Then there are the unavoidable boss's orders, executive demands, new corporate policies, and project guidelines, all of which need to be "actioned real time". And of course, all of this is "streamlined" by the latest network architecture and business software (which doubtlessly requires more professional-development courses). In this way, while the bureaucratic and administrative apparatus of the modern office pays lip service to efficiency, it frequently just promotes information overload and apportions busywork.

The upshot of these changes is that we are awash in bits and bytes of bullshit. This is often called an "information economy", but the market is supposed to run on scarcity, not surplus. In reality, it's an "attention economy" – what is in short supply are the mental and physical resources for actually taking notice of anything and for trying to make sense of it. But companies need consumers to concentrate on their products, and staff on their memorandums and policies. As a result of this, public relations, communications and advertising executives are continually inventing new ways to excite, stimulate and harass, all with the intention of garnering as much attention as possible for their product, proposal or press release. In advertising especially, this resembles a miniature arms race, where each "hook" is more absurd than the last (one clothing advertisement reads: "Diesel: Global Warming Ready"). The result is a war for the territory of our minds, where we're bombarded at work and home with the most vulgar, extreme or intense messages, all competing for our eyes and ears.

Another cause of exhaustion and frustration in the workplace is the new "flexible" workforce, often on casual rates or short-term contracts. By dumping jobs for life, companies make themselves leaner, lighter and faster. They're not stuck with the "dead wood" of permanent staff, and they can relocate quickly when the labour's too expensive (or the shareholders need a quick dividend). Of course, this can be a boon for workers, as can "flexitime" – for confident, assertive staff it can make the home–life juggle less painful. But for many young and vulnerable workers, it's another sacrifice. They still do the same hack work, but they miss the job continuity, peer recognition and affirming fraternity (as well as the bonuses and leave entitlements). And they're also likely to be coerced into obedience – it's hard to rock the boat when you're begging for a contract to be renewed or your shifts to be maintained. This makes money well enough, but it leaves many in the workforce uncertain, anxious and insecure. They end up exhausting themselves with unpaid overtime, and working when they're ill (often infecting their colleagues as they do). Absurdly, there's even a word for this: "presenteeism" – the opposite of absenteeism. It's hardly the judicious use of the workday Franklin was endorsing. At best, this trivializes work; at worst, it transforms it into a depressing, draining burden. This is, as Marx put it, "a labour of self-sacrifice, of mortification".

For the American philosopher John Dewey, writing in the 1930s, the acceleration of life was dangerous – it's simply contrary to our nature to work so hard, so fast and for so little reward (physical or existential, as much as pecuniary). Dewey pointed out that humans – like all living things – are tightly interwoven with their environment. To survive, we engage in an ongoing to and fro with it, whether this is tracking trails, foraging for food and building shelter, or driving, shopping and renovating. We act upon the world, and it acts upon us. Dewey called this whole congress with the world "experience", and each little part "an experience". These experiences have their own rhythm: a beginning, a middle and an end, departure and arrival, start and finish. Preparing meals, driving, writing and countless other everyday tasks have their cycles and patterns, where they come to fruition: we serve the pasta, we park in the driveway, or we cap off the final sentence. Dewey notes that we genuinely enjoy these climaxes – as he put it, "moments of fulfilment punctuate experience with rhythmically enjoyed intervals". In other words, part of a fulfilling life is the ability and opportunity to see things through – little things like shopping lists and games, or big things like work projects and renovations. By entering into the rhythms of life, we gain immeasurable pleasure, and this is precisely the cadence sought by T. S. Eliot in poetry and employment.

Importantly, there is no one rhythm. Love affairs burn, smoulder and cool over the years, while fights can rage and peter out in minutes. Artists have rhythms of work – Simone de Beauvoir began the workday with a cup of tea, wrote from ten until one o'clock, lunched, and then worked again from five o'clock until nine. Joan Miro locked himself in his studio, worked five hours a day, and then boxed at a local gym. Daily routines are wedded to those of brushstrokes and mood – Henri Matisse hummed dance-hall tunes as he worked. Poets work with the beat of intonation and accent, and the tempo of the syllables. Fiction writers are especially sensitive to the cadence of plot and prose. Life itself has rhythm: the cycles of daily nutrition and waste, reproduction and decay. Because of this, all organisms have their own time – from the centuries of the old-growth forest to the days of the gadfly. Time is not an "endless and uniform flow", wrote Dewey in *Art as Experience*, but "the rhythmic ebb and flow of expectant impulse, forward and retracted movement, resistance and suspense". Everything has its own pace, tempo and span, and our moments of joy are often tightly bound up in these.

To Dewey's dismay, human contentment is frequently quashed in the modern workplace. In the spirit of Franklin, the narrow goal of productivity standardizes all rhythms into a single calculable time, increasing the speed of almost every office, factory and employee. Dewey argued that this results in a working life where the present enjoyment of labour is sacrificed to future production (whether it's a widget, a report, or "quality customer service"). Instead of being rewarding for its own sake – like the rhythmic craft of the writer, painter or potter – this labour is merely a means to an end. These ends are defined and imposed by bosses and managers, while everything else (from raw resources to equipment to workers) is treated as "instruments", to be organized for the sake of maximum yield and minimum cost. Men and machines are then set to run as quickly as possible. With his typical optimism, Dewey wanted employees to enjoy their daily routines, but he feared that all too many were "in enslavement to keeping the machines going at an increasingly rapid rate".

As we've seen, the irony is that acceleration is often a barrier to productive work. This is partly because there are so many demands and so little time. Automated technologies have afforded a great many time savings, but they also create an atmosphere of urgency and immediate outputs, instead of patient, engaged attention. They transform the workplace into a site for the harried production of tomorrow's profit, rather than for today's professional competency and completion. The pleasure of challenging work for its own sake is deferred, and rarely achieved. So profit-driven acceleration not only fragments the rhythms of the day but can also leave employees disappointed, irritated and lacking in genuine motivation – they don't enjoy the precious "moments of fulfilment" that Dewey described and which Eliot enjoyed. Frustrated by cut corners and half-done jobs, and fatigued by short deadlines and accelerated workflow, many no longer see work as a rewarding and enriching occupation. Instead, it's simply a way to pay the bills. There's nothing wrong with paying the bills – but it shouldn't be the only reward for the effort, stress and lost hours that most jobs entail.

For Dewey, the great tragedy wasn't simply that the emancipatory potential of work was wasted. It was also that "free time" was contaminated in the process. Because it's opposed to professional life, which is serious and important, free time becomes a kind of pointless play or desperate refuelling; what Dewey described in *Human Nature and Conduct* as "a feverish hurry for diversion, excitement, display, otherwise there is no leisure except a sudden torpor". For him, this was the inevitable consequence of work understood as a mere instrument of profit and productivity: employment deprived of enjoyment, and "free time" robbed of anything genuinely creative and constructive: of its "freedom". In this way, Franklin's adage corrupts the home as it conquers the business world. By disrupting the rhythms of life, the modern workplace also transforms domesticity, making it a site for rushed fun or vegetative stupor.

The point of Dewey's criticism isn't that hard work is bad or that employment is always vulgar exploitation. Often our desire for accomplishment or status coincides with the profit motive – we gain recognition and fulfilment as we make money for ourselves, and the company. And as Eliot's life implied, our guilt, pride or loneliness can become spurs to rewarding employment – they lead to professional esteem and satisfaction instead of misadventure. But all too often, the priorities of the modern workplace are at odds with these aims. The conflict begins when businesses emphasize tomorrow's profit and productivity over today's professional satisfaction. The experience of work becomes faster, less personal and more fragmented. For many, the job is no longer a rewarding occupation and becomes a banal preoccupation, to be uncaringly dealt with and shrugged off. This mood of dissatisfaction intensifies as new technologies and unrealistic expectations disrupt the very rhythms that allow for workplace contentment. While Franklin saw mankind as a "toolmaker", perhaps he didn't foresee an age when the tools of work would rob it of its joy (he was, after all, an industrialist), or when pecuniary interests would lead to indifferent idleness. Dewey's assessment suggests that, if time is money, we need to re-evaluate what we do with both. We might use our wages to secure free time: hours for the cultivation of liberty.

Free time and liberty

Employment offers a promise of human fulfilment that is rarely attained. For many of us it's a barrier to health and happiness instead of a path to achievement and contentment. But labour can't easily be dispensed with, in favour of a life of breezy idleness or abject hedonism ("as soon as there is no physical or other coercion," said

Marx, "labor is avoided like the plague"). We have to work, often for bosses and businesses we don't hold in high esteem. We might have a vision of Marx's "creative labour" but we have mouths and mortgages to feed. What this calls for is not desperation or recrimination but judicious compromise – we need to make the best of the limitations the world provides. Sometimes, this means working in jobs that are menial or uncreative, but making the best use of our free time as something genuinely free.

A wonderful example is the Dutch philosopher Benedict de Spinoza (also known by his Hebrew name Baruch, or "blessed"). Next to the much documented Marx and Eliot, we know relatively little about him, but what we do know is fascinating. Spinoza was one of the most important thinkers of the Enlightenment, making highly original contributions to our ideas of God, nature and freedom. As his scholarly peers were luminaries like Descartes, Hobbes, Locke, Newton and Leibniz, this is no small feat. He was also an influence on some of the greatest philosophers of the modern world, including Kant, Hegel and Nietzsche. In a letter to a friend, posted from Sils-Maria in Switzerland, Nietzsche wrote of Spinoza: "I am utterly amazed, utterly enchanted! I have a *precursor*, and what a precursor!" It wasn't only philosophers who lauded the great Jewish thinker. In 1920, Albert Einstein visited Spinoza's house in Amsterdam, afterwards writing a poem in his honour: "How much do I love that noble man / More than I could tell with words / I fear though he'll remain alone / With a holy halo of his own." Even if the poetry is doggerel, the sentiment is clear: Spinoza was an illuminating, inspiring scholar.

Yet Spinoza never worked in a university. He subsisted on his craft as a lens grinder and occasionally received money from friends. Of course, he was no ordinary lens maker – the Dutch mathematician Huygens said his "most excellent" lenses had an "admirable polish" and Leibniz called him "an outstanding optician". Nonetheless, that a philosopher of Spinoza's calibre worked outside academia is significant in itself. Nowadays, it is rare to find an eminent scholar who isn't ensconced in a university. Even if it's an emeritus position with a few handy perks, most thinkers seek the safety and security of the cloisters. But Spinoza wasn't a philosopher-in-exile, shivering at the gates of academia – he quite deliberately shunned it.

In 1673, a letter arrived that might have remedied his professional isolation. It was written by Professor J. Ludwig Fabricius, an academic at Heidelberg University, and it was essentially a job offer. Despite his trifling academic career, Spinoza was to enjoy an annual salary equal to that of professors and was assured "ample freedom of teaching". On behalf of the university and regional authorities, Fabricius promised Spinoza "a life worthy of a philosopher".

Like most philosophers, then and now, Spinoza was probably flattered by this generous offer. Heidelberg was a once-great European university, and Karl Ludwig, the enlightened Elector of the region, was trying to regain its former glory. The professorship would have given Spinoza wealth, status and security, and he would have enjoyed a place in an "illustrious university", his great philosophical works well in the public eye.

Yet this publicity was precisely what the Jewish philosopher feared. Less than two months after sending his letter, Professor Fabricius had Spinoza's reply. In it, he wrote that he did not trust "men's various dispositions and contradictions", and feared that his public position at Heidelberg would lead to all sorts of religious quarrels. Moreover, he did not want to give up his philosophical research in favour of "teaching young students". He entreated the professor: "You see, distinguished Sir, that I am not holding back in the hope of getting something better, but through my love of quietness, which I think I can in some measure secure, if I keep away from lecturing in public." In other words, Spinoza declined the university job because his free-time and philosophy were more valuable than fame and fortune at Heidelberg – academia was a distraction from his work.

Now, perhaps Spinoza was too stubborn to work in different ways or at different times. Perhaps he was simply weak – after all, his contemporary Descartes spent most of the day in bed (and reputedly died when the Queen of Sweden made him rise early on cold Scandinavian mornings). But Spinoza wasn't some shrinking violet, in retreat from the cruel world. In 1672, the year before he was offered the Heidelberg post, Spinoza was horrified and angered by the lynching and bloody murder of the Dutch statesmen the de Witt brothers. In *The Black Tulip*, Alexander Dumas described the scene: "after having mangled, and torn, and completely stripped the two brothers, the mob dragged their naked and bloody bodies to an extemporised gibbet, where amateur executioners hung them up by the feet". Spinoza was mortified, and his "love of quietness" did not stop him making a placard that read "You are the greatest of barbarians", which he intended to put up at the site of the massacre. Leibniz, who spoke with him shortly after, said that Spinoza was only prevented from mounting the placard by his host, who locked the doors of the house. This suggests not only that Spinoza was more than able to withstand stress and scrutiny of a sort (for his religious beliefs, in particular) but also that he might have benefited from a sojourn away from unfriendly Amsterdam.

Yet he didn't leave the Netherlands, and he kept grinding and polishing his lenses. Four years after sending his letter to Fabricius, Spinoza was dead, at the age of forty-five – he was killed by tuberculosis, worsened by the glass dust of his lens grinding. And in his death lies a disturbing but otherwise rudimentary truth. Like most of us, Spinoza had no economic safety net. His free time was guaranteed only by his lens grinding: a secure and stable job, which gave him the freedom he needed for his philosophical studies. Perhaps he loved his glass craft – his pieces were certainly admired, demonstrating dedication and care. It's likely that, in his renowned lenses, we see Spinoza "contemplating himself in a world he created" (as Marx would have endorsed). But the justification for his trade, the rationale with which he passed up a Heidelberg professorship, was his philosophy: he wanted to preserve his free time for thinking and writing. At the end of the day, it was logic, ethics and metaphysics that inspired him, not glass and grinders. In a way, his commitment to philosophy cost Spinoza his life.

Wading through most of his works, many readers (laymen and scholars) might be surprised by this. Without the flair of Nietzsche, or the grumpy hectoring of Marx, Spinoza's masterworks were logical yawn-fests. Arranged as a series of seemingly unending axioms, definitions, propositions and objections (the so-called "geometric" method), they're not enjoyable reading. "Everything which is, is either in itself or another," he wrote in his *Ethics*. There's something tedious and pedantic in Spinoza's great works – they resemble a dull workplace rather than sublime adventures in thought. And there is something disturbingly mechanical in his geometric method. Yet his finest philosophical writings weren't stifling at all – on the contrary, they vigorously championed liberty.

In the twenty-first century – an era in which "freedom" and "liberty" are fodder for advertising ("Jeep Liberty 2003 Freedom Edition") – it's important to be clear on what this meant for Spinoza. As it happens, he gave a very quick and easy definition of freedom in his *Ethics*. He said that something is free when it "exists solely by the necessity of its own nature, and of which the action is determined by itself alone". In other words, we are free when we are authoritatively being ourselves and not deferring to the demands or expectations of someone (or something) else. And this implies that liberty requires a robust and self-sufficient character. We can't be free until we've cultivated an "I" that can resist the demands of others, one that has its own modus operandi. For Spinoza, the path to this "I" was philosophy.

In his unfinished treatise *On the Improvement of the Understanding*, Spinoza explained what led him to this epiphany. He bluntly stated that he had had a gutful of the "futility" of his social life. Most men were seeking pleasure, riches or fame, and each was a doomed enterprise. Pleasure was fleeting, he said – it dulled the mind, and led to melancholy. Wealth and status were nice, but celebrities and rich men just wanted more cash and adoration (how we've progressed). Their cravings were always unsatisfied, and they wasted themselves trying to satisfy them. Meanwhile, their happiness was at the whims of others anyway – "It compels its votaries," he said of his successful peers, "to order their lives according to the opinions of their fellow men, shunning what they usually shun, and seeking what they usually seek." Spinoza's picture is of a throng of otherwise ordinary men, tossed to and fro by accident, want or whimsy.

Trying to avoid this malaise, Spinoza the lens grinder sought happiness in freedom. This wasn't an abstract freedom, circumscribed by the law, but a definite and deliberate liberty of the mind. As he saw it, instead of being compelled by fortune, the mind is designed (by God, of course) to obey its own laws. It doesn't have to bow to chance and chaos – it patiently stays its own course. In this way, it overcomes evils and finds good.

In a heretical stroke (he was excommunicated by his synagogue), Spinoza spoke of good and evil in very secular, modern terms. There was no absolute table of divine ticks and crosses: good was whatever kept us stable, secure and strong, and evil all that unsettled or weakened us. The good couldn't be attained by proclivities and inclinations, as these are illogical and uncertain. The only way to achieve a robust character (and gain freedom) was to be consciously and carefully rational; to seek the perfect and eternal instead of the defective and decayed. We can then lay down rules of life, which will keep us happy and healthy. If money and fame help, so be it – but if they are mistaken for goods, they will warp our minds and leave us to the whims of fate and fickle men. While the ignorant man is "distracted in various ways by external causes", he explained in *Ethics*, "how potent is the wise man".

The implications of Spinoza's emphasis on liberty are elegant and clarifying. For Spinoza, freedom was intimately related to sustained, self-directed attention. It wasn't simply the absence of violent coercion, or a matter of rights and other legalities. In fact, liberty wasn't something that other individuals or institutions could provide – it was up to the wise man, and him alone, to properly cultivate himself. The philosopher's ideal was the ability to avoid accidental diversions and deliberate subterfuge, and the facility to attend perceptively and thoughtfully to what was worthwhile. In other words, Spinoza's ideal of freedom was a life without distraction.

Perhaps the Enlightenment scholar put too much faith in universal and eternal ideas, or the transparent and faithful workings of our intelligence. But we needn't agree with all of his philosophy to glean vital truths from his life and scholarship. He had a sharp eye for what he needed; what would make him (as opposed to others) flourish. He knew he had to be a speculative philosopher and was willing to put his nose to the grindstone for it (quite literally). Taken alongside his diligent craftsmanship, this suggests that what is crucial is a stable and clarifying vision of what's healthy (or "good", as Spinoza would have it) and the presence of mind to seek it patiently and judiciously.

It is not always so simple to achieve these things, nor is it easy to give up employment altogether. This is why Spinoza needed his lens grinding, with its safe income and reliable hours. Even if it had moments of banality, or injurious equipment, it gave him a genuine opportunity to seek freedom. This is what we might call "waged liberty": it's the recognition that we sometimes *need* money and esteem (professional or public) but that these are only the means to an end. They afford the security to think coherently about what we need and to develop the wherewithal to act on it. And they provide the leisure hours to do so without infuriating distraction. The implication is this: work isn't always free, but it can fuel our emancipation.

In this, Spinoza's life offers an example of the transformation of everyday work into something more ambitious. And his example has broader implications for us today. Spinoza sought the rigour of scholarly enlightenment – we might hurl ourselves into literature, history, sport, gardening, painting or music. The issue is not the specific preoccupation but the general spirit of civilized curiosity. What's vital is to seek rewarding leisure, leisure that attunes our attention, cultivates our intellect and inspires our imagination – not simply in the office or shop or factory (because this is often impossible) but in the remaining hours of free time. These offer us the opportunity and the inclination to be clearer about what we want in life and give us the mental resources to achieve it. We might not always have Marx's creative labour, or Eliot's discipline, but we can have real free time: for the judicious cultivation of liberty.

Child's play

In *Thus Spoke Zarathustra*, Nietzsche wrote of the "three metamorphoses of the spirit". The spirit becomes a camel, the camel a lion, and the lion a child. In this tiny little parable is the dilemma of modern work. The camel bears the burdens of life – it suffers, endures and struggles. In this way, it faces necessity, and grows stronger and more patient as it does. However, eventually the camel grows tired of bearing the burdens of its master. It trudges out into the desert and decides to carry its own burdens. It becomes a lion, for only the lion has the ferocity and strength to say no to the master and demand its own freedom. Yet the lion can only fight – it cannot "create new values", says Nietzsche. To be truly free, the lion becomes a child, for only a child can see the world with new eyes, and start again freely. The child is, as Nietzsche puts it, "all innocence and forgetfulness, a new beginning, a sport". Like a child in play we discover what is the highest and most joyous about ourselves. In the modern workplace, these three metamorphoses remain a challenge for us all: to endure busywork and its distractions, to fiercely say no to subjugation, and to claim the leisurely freedom of the child.

3. The reins of necessity

> From the moment I left the house and got into the car, I have been writing this letter. And now, late at night, I cannot write after all. (I am using a typewriter because my fountain pen is broken and my handwriting has become illegible.)
> (Hannah Arendt, letter to Martin Heidegger, 9 February 1950)

A few years ago, my wife and I enjoyed a long holiday in Greece. After the sweat and smog of ancient Athens, we took a ferry to the Ionian Islands, nestled off the west coast of Greece, not far from southern Italy. Our destination was the mythic island of Odysseus: Ithaca. Not many people know about Ithaca, perhaps because party isles like Santorini have given boozy Anglo-Saxon revellers all the sun and *souvlaki* they crave. Ithaca is beautiful, but not because of its nude beaches, cheap alcohol, or sunburnt Londoners. Instead, Ithaca weds the hardiness of scrubby olive groves and ancient stone walls to the delicate pinks and reds of wild cyclamen flowers and the quiet lapping of a turquoise sea. Half an hour's mad winding taxi-ride from end to end, the whole tiny island is as Homer wrote in *The Odyssey*: "a rugged land, too cramped for driving horses".

On one beautiful autumn afternoon, my wife and I were taken by a friend to a little village in the mountains of Ithaca, called Exoghi. The village was strangely deserted, save for a few old women. Houses destroyed by an earthquake decades before still lay in ruins, and cats roamed. While a little melancholic, the village was also full of life: grape vines bearing fat green and purple fruit rambled around stone walls, trellises and an old almond tree. After a lunch of grapes and freshly baked bread we trekked back down the mountain to the breathtaking Aphales Bay: cool lapis lazuli glinting amid bright chalk cliffs. We passed a cemetery on the mountain's edge, with its bleached bone-white crosses shining against the blue water. This cliff-top resting place was pure poetry. Grinning like children, we left the cemetery and headed for the cool cypress forests that grow on the side of the mountain.

Then it happened: my mobile phone rang. The white cliffs, the herbs, the sunlight and sea – all these blessings slowly dimmed as I was wrenched out of my reverie. Annoyed and mildly embarrassed, I answered it. It was my mother. From the moment I answered the phone to the moment I ended the call, I have absolutely no memory of where I was or what I was doing. I forgot all about the plants growing wild by the side of the road, the gorgeous views of Aphales Bay, or the dusty path we followed to the shores below – these images come from a photo I took later. I was completely sidetracked by the person ringing me from some 15,000 kilometres away in Australia. I am reminded of the old joke about Christopher Columbus. As he steps onto the soil of the New World after months at sea, one of the natives hands him an envelope. Absolutely baffled, he opens it and reads: "What kind of a son are you? They don't have letter boxes in the Atlantic?"

But I must be honest: the fault wasn't my mother's, it was mine. I had every opportunity to avoid the call, from leaving my phone at the *pension* to smashing it in half and binning the digital nagger. Yet I didn't do any of these things – in fact, they never even occurred to me. Answering the phone was an uncontrollable and unconscious reflex. It was as though I had been trained to hear the ring tone and immediately take the call – primed to react to the stimulus like one of Pavlov's salivating Borzoi. When it was on, so was I. Worse still, I *needed* it; I longed for its promise of novelty and surprise. In this sense, something slightly more sinister was happening than absent-mindedness. Far from being a simple digital convenience, my mobile phone had become an addiction: it was a "hit" I couldn't refuse. And this was why I was so easily distracted, even among the beauties of Ithaca.

The technological habit

I'm not the only digital junkie. This mechanical compulsion is one of the most striking aspects of modern life. All over the world, perfectly reasonable adults find themselves unable to live without gadgets – the morning's train journey is a Dantesque punishment without an MP3-playing camera phone; a day without MySpace or Facebook "friends" is solitary confinement. And it's not only our leisure time that's distracted; the workplace is a hotbed of technological obsession. The *Guardian* newspaper recently described a psychological study that investigated the effects of email on British workers. Astonishingly, it reported that the "distractions of constant emails, text and phone messages are a greater threat to IQ and concentration than taking cannabis". The survey found that volunteers for the experiments were stupefied and muddled, as if they were hitting the spliffs on a Saturday night. Instead of focusing on their jobs, they were awaiting their next emails, and interrupting conversations to check their screens. (This gives high internet use a whole new meaning.)

Electronic addiction has been intensified by portable computers such as the BlackBerry, Palm Pilot, Palm Treo and others. "I use it all the time, constantly," said white-collar worker David Brereton in one newspaper interview. The IT professional was conscious of his dependence but was unable to shake it. "When I hear it vibrating during dinner, I think, 'I'll ignore that'," he said. "But within a couple of minutes I'm up and checking what it was. My wife gets a little bit frustrated because if a message comes in I find myself not being able to resist."

Recently, an American colleague of my father sat in a hotel restaurant, beaming with relief at the thirty emails on his BlackBerry instead of the usual seventy. What's illuminating isn't simply the ridiculous number of communiqués but his choice to read them during breakfast. Despite his resentment at so many emails, he still turned the device on. Even the most intimate meal was accompanied by the beeping, flashing, vibrating little friend. Meanwhile, stories of laptops, mobile phones and BlackBerrys interrupting romantic dinners and sex are too numerous to be funny. (Not all vibrating bedroom toys are good for our sex life.)

BlackBerry in the bedroom, mobile phone calls on the porcelain throne, wireless hotspots in the café – this is distraction twenty-first century style: we can't give our attention to what's worthwhile because we're drawn to the mysterious allure of the machine. Importantly, this doesn't mean we're irrevocably brainwashed, the unthinking masses of counterculture stereotypes. We're certainly capable of doing otherwise. But what's so striking is that we so frequently don't, because our psyche is quietly captured.

Confronted by this assault on our volition, it's tempting to respond with indignant fury – it would be so very satisfying (for me, at least) to make iPods illegal, bury all mobile phones in the Mariana Trench and arrest Bill Gates. ("You are guilty, Mr Gates, of crimes against the Queen's English.") But we need to be wary of self-righteous technophobia. There is nothing intrinsically wrong with tools: manual, mechanical or digital. From the majesty of the Egyptian pyramids to the intriguing beauty of modern cinema, technology has enabled some of our finest scientific, artistic and scholarly achievements. And more importantly, machines are crucial to our modern way of life. Any attempt to return to a pre-modern paradise would mean giving up everything from aeroplane travel to word processing and cancer research. If we esteem the civilization that these afford, any escape from technology will be counterproductive. To recover from the distractions of the technological age, what's required is not Luddite extremism but a more ambitious relationship to our tools – one that promotes our liberty instead of weakening it.

Ananke, faceless goddess

A helpful place to begin is with the ancient Greek philosopher Aristotle. Aristotle esteemed technology – for him, it was indispensable for freedom. "No man can live well, or indeed live at all," he wrote in his *Politics*, "unless he be provided with necessaries." By this, he meant the basics of life: shelter, food and water, companionship. And "instruments" were crucial in providing these.

However, when Aristotle spoke of "instruments", he did not just mean the water well and the olive press. He also meant the slaves who fetched the water or collected the olive oil. Foreign as it might seem to modern eyes, to Aristotle slaves were just living tools – they provided the basics of life. They were owned and used just as we own and use dishwashers and refrigerators today. In fact, Aristotle thought that machines might one day replace slaves. Dreaming of instruments that could move and think on their own, he said: "if every instrument could accomplish its own work, obeying or anticipating the will of others … chief workmen would not want servants, nor masters slaves". Obviously, Aristotle's idle fancy has become our everyday reality – we have instruments that work automatically, switch on and off when we are not around, and generally chug away on their own steam. In other words, our modern machines do the work of yesteryear's slaves: they deal with brutal necessity.

The word *necessity* may be a little dull to our ears, but it meant something more powerful and menacing to the Greeks. While their

Olympian gods were like men of flesh and bone, there was one goddess with neither body nor face: Ananke. The Romans called her "Necessitas" and she was the dark mother of the Fates. In English, we call her "Necessity". The goddess Ananke did not have temples or priests, because no prayers, no offerings, no sacrifices could change what was necessary. In the simple words of Italian author Roberto Calasso, "What could one ask of she who does not listen?" In Aeschylus's noble play *Prometheus Bound*, we learn that even mighty Zeus, king of the gods, "cannot fly from Fate". Ananke is the steady march of time, and the toothy white grin of the Grim Reaper. While we all must confront these, there are also the numerous everyday necessities: the options to kill or be killed, eat or starve, build walls or be invaded.

In Aristotle's time, it was the slaves who had to deal with many of these. While he and his well-off chums lived a life of liberty, the slaves cooked and cleaned every day, only to see more mess and hunger the next day. Like mythic Sisyphus pushing his boulder up a hill for eternity, their pains came to nothing and their words and deeds were swallowed up by time. As philosopher Hannah Arendt writes, "the slave's degradation was ... a fate worse than death, because it carried with it a metamorphosis of man into something akin to a tame animal". Arendt's point is important, because it reveals an instinctive wariness of necessity – it's somehow dangerous for human independence. As we adapt to its endless rhythms, it threatens to encroach upon our liberty.

In the Judeo–Christian civilization that succeeded paganism, necessity also inspired fear and obedience. The character of Jehovah in the Old Testament was a fearsome, wrathful God whose will was one of absolute necessity. Just as Ananke for the Greeks was seen as a faceless, relentless deity, so too was the Lord an invisible, unyielding force. Abraham *must* kill Isaac, and Noah *must* build his ark – this necessity was in the form of a command or interdiction, where disobedience was a discordance with the cosmos itself.

As Hellenic philosophy transformed Judaism into Christianity, this divine rule was reinterpreted not only as an order but as a cosmic law. Despite the Christian emphasis on love and grace, the essential character of God as an inexorable cosmic lawgiver remained. For Thomas Aquinas, the mind of God was the basic law of all things – God was not part of the world of chance and contingency but the ultimate necessity of all things. While men, for Aquinas, were free, they were free only insofar as God's necessity granted them freedom – "He is the cause of this very thing in them," wrote the Angelic Doctor in the thirteenth century. Put simply, God's freedom was the necessity of the universe – and God was someone to be feared.

Over the centuries, though, necessity ceased to be a cosmic villain or sacred law. With the advent of modern mathematical science, necessity was domesticated. One of the cornerstones of maths is necessity: 1 plus 1 can't equal 2 just occasionally, or whenever the 1s feel like it; they must equal 2 all the time. And this logic is essential to almost every mathematical operation – each step must follow logically from the other, or the equation is invalid and irrational. In the sixteenth and seventeenth centuries, mathematics was incorporated into the heart of scientific theory and experiment. The idea wasn't simply that numerical laws were heavenly miracles but that the fabric of the cosmos was itself mathematical. The great Italian astronomer Galileo Galilei wrote, "Philosophy is written in this great book – I mean the universe – which ... is written in the language of mathematics, and its characters are triangles, circles, and the geometric figures." The notion of a Divine Law – as found in theology – was slowly transformed into the mathematical laws of "natural philosophy", what we call science today. While these laws couldn't be changed or avoided, they could be mastered.

For philosophers and scientists, mathematical expertise was wondrous. The mind could follow each step from beginning to end, and could work out universal rules of nature and spirit. In the work of Kant, for example, we embraced our freedom by obeying moral necessity. To be ethical was to work without contingency, without inclination, and to choose only the most universal and eternal moral laws. In the logic of Hegel, the entire edifice of thought was self-necessitating – if followed perfectly, its final conclusions led back to its beginnings. Even if these thinkers disdained the scientific deference to "stuff", they shared Galileo's love of mathematical necessity: to master logic was to master the essence of life.

Hand in hand with experimental science and abject economic imperatives, the tale of modern technology is a story of this increasing mastery. And with every increase in calculating speed and accuracy, our sovereignty increases – we get closer to reading the mind of God. As we do so, our machines take the place of nature. Instead of encountering the necessity of weather and seasons, and the limits of our weak and vulnerable bodies, we live very much in a world where machines and their products are our environment. The upshot of this is that we don't have the same fear or anxiety about natural necessity, because it's our machines that face Ananke's relentless rules. They tirelessly wash and dry our clothes, ferry us to work and school, and carry our words across the globe. They work in extreme heat and cold, day and night, year after year, with neither complaint nor lamentation. (Just before I wrote this, my microwave politely told me to enjoy my meal.)

All over the modern world, we're enjoying the benefits of this progress. We're capable of harnessing enormous amounts of energy over vast distances, with a degree of precision undreamt of a hundred years ago, let alone in Aristotle's time. The affluence and influence of developed nations are partly driven by this technological mastery – our factories, transport, financial calculations and innovation. And the engine of all this is necessity – Ananke is the patron goddess of the modern age. But as the Greeks suspected, there is something uncivilized in this faceless divinity: the very real possibility of diminished freedom.

A second nature

Today, Aristotle's mechanical slaves are a banal reality: homes, high-rise offices and sprawling cities are serviced by sophisticated machines that regulate our room temperature, facilitate our conversations, coordinate our transportation. But this commonplace domination can go both ways: the more we mechanize our lives, the more we ourselves fall in line. Just as the Athenian servants were shaped by necessity, so too does technological necessity regulate our bodies and standardize our minds. And this can be deceptively comfortable. In a world of mechanical necessity, life's engine runs very smoothly – but we're no longer at the wheel. This is precisely why we can be so distracted; gently hypnotized by the very rhythms we have invented.

A wonderful allegory of technological distraction comes from *England*, the travel journal of the Greek writer Nikos Kazantzakis, author of *Zorba the Greek*. Awed by the grandeur and decay of Britain, Kazantzakis visited the industrial cities of Birmingham, Liverpool, Manchester and Sheffield. Amazed and terrified, he was encountering the effects of technological Ananke. He saw the misery of the factory workers and the grime and soot of coal-fired business. In *England*, he wrote of "wretched human beings", "faces grim and fraught with grief", and the endlessly rotating wheel of labour, exhaustion and filth.

Yet Kazantzakis was not a backward Luddite yearning for an ancient age of medieval horses and carts. He didn't hate technology. Instead, he saw it as a way to better ourselves – to increase the strength and reach of the human spirit. He wrote: "The purpose of the machine was to be a steed for the spirit to mount so that the spirit could pursue its chimera – pursue it not by idle wishing but by practical methods." However, at some point the rider and his mount lost their way. "The horses," wrote Kazantzakis, "gradually mounted the riders."

This is a striking metaphor, but what exactly does this "mounting" look like? And why does it happen so easily? A helpful analysis comes from philosopher Herbert Marcuse. For Marcuse, technological oppression wasn't accidental; it was crucial to modern society. In *One Dimensional Man*, he spoke of technology as a "higher rationality", not because it was more civilized (precisely the opposite), but because its mathematical logic was more advanced than old kinds of exploitation. Instead of the fairly rudimentary medieval relationships – where a lord steals from a peasant, the peasant steals from his neighbour, and they all kick the pigs – modern oppression was instantiated in machinery and in the "divine language" praised by Galileo. It became a worldwide grid of connections between bosses and workers, the bullies and the bullied, paparazzi and celebrities. Instead of praising God or gods, there's a religious deference to the "objective order of things", where this means essentially the existing system of telecommunications, transport and factories, and the 24-hour markets they serve. The entire edifice of modern machines (and their tangle of connections) comes to look like a kind of commonsense reality, which can neither be tinkered with nor questioned. And at the bottom of it, for Marcuse, is this iron steed, technology. It allows people to manipulate, punish and pry, but from afar, and with the sterile objectivity of the digital implement. "The new modes of aggression," wrote Marcuse, "destroy without getting one's hands dirty, one's body soiled, one's mind incriminated."

In simple terms, Marcuse was suggesting something quite counterintuitive. For many, technology is progressive: its leaps of insight and innovation lead to ever-increasing comfort and leisure. And perhaps more importantly, machines are supposedly neutral – they have no vested interests, no quirky psychological foibles. But Marcuse's theory maintains that, despite this, technology is violent, aggressive and destructive. As the "objective order of things", it quite brutally organizes society. It shuttles the exploited to labour or war, and delivers profit to the elite. It's the email server that exhausts workers, and the cable television that blares day and night. And more importantly, it's the basic logic of necessity underneath all this – the taken-for-granted urgency and relentlessness – that marks the modern era.

For Marcuse, necessity wasn't simply a passing political or social contrivance – a transient feature of the "outside world", like the weather. Instead, he argued, it transforms consciousness. In the guise of science, management, infrastructure and economics, it is internalized. It becomes, as he put it, "a mode of thought and behaviour which is immune against any other than the established reality". Its chief characteristic is a blindness to imagination and reflection, which defers to the status quo. Basic questions of "What?" and "Why?" are replaced by the practicalities of "How?"; with cause, effect and their chains of necessity. Marcuse's point wasn't that we are unintelligent or brutal, but that we understandably absorb what surrounds us, what regulates our day-to-day lives. And technological rationality, as he put it, "organises the whole", the ensemble of society and psyche. The result is an inability to resist, to imagine alternatives, to invent new possibilities of identity and belief.

In this way, the necessity of technology infuses our awareness – not wholly, but enough to diminish our freedom. Technology quite literally becomes second nature: it manages the world around us, and transforms our mental and physical reflexes. We let our computers sort, prioritize, categorize and file. At home we allow ourselves to be sucked into pointless banter (complete with advertisements), and at work we adapt to the office's mechanical cadence (ramped up to ensure profit). Our everyday road crossings and lift journeys are coordinated by computers calculating. Our taxation, welfare and employment are mediated by often clumsy databases. And when governed in this way, consciousness loses its spontaneity and assertion, and it becomes more pliant. Instead of inventing its own rhythms and cadences, it awaits the next signal, icon or flashing light. (When the "random" setting on your iPod is as close as you get to spontaneity, you know you're in trouble.) This is a chief cause of so many day-to-day distractions – we defer to mechanical necessity, instead of forging our own.

Heidegger's hut

In the face of technology's intrusions, flight is a forgivable response. For anyone with a Romantic disposition, it's reasonable to urge a retreat from demonic technology – an exodus to the wilderness, or a long-lost Eden. And certainly, there is something affirming in the experience of fresh air and simplicity, away from the hum of machines. This is partly why so many of us turn to gardening, go hiking or go jogging around lakes and parks. But there's something hypocritical at the heart of most Romantic technophobes – an unwillingness to recognize their own dependence on the fruits of technology.

A wonderful example of retreat is provided by the German philosopher Martin Heidegger. For many today, Heidegger was the finest example of someone who counselled a return to pre-modern life – while enjoying intercontinental travel, international publishing and a ski hut only technology could erect. And worse still, Heidegger's political allies, the Nazis, were themselves enamoured of technology, from radar to the promise of nuclear weapons. But at the same time, Heidegger's theories remain some of the most penetrating accounts of technology. More importantly, in Heidegger's own compromises, we can see a glimpse of how we might manage the iron horse of technology. In the grey area between his philosophy and his life, it's possible to discern a middle way, one that recognizes the benefits of technology, while focusing our attention on the vital cultivation of human potentiality. This not only serves to alleviate the bugbear of distraction but also suggests how we might live more freely.

Like many, Heidegger felt imprisoned by technology. In a 1935 lecture entitled "An Introduction to Metaphysics", Heidegger surveyed Western history and contemporary ills from the standpoint of Being. (Being was like an old tune Heidegger hummed his whole life.) The students attending his lecture, at Freiburg University near Germany's Black Forest, might have expected a dry analysis of what it is to "be" – and they weren't disappointed. But Heidegger also treated them to an absolute corker of a rant about modern life and technology. Treating the United States and Soviet Union as equally dismal, he spoke of a time "when the farthermost corner of the globe has been conquered by technology and opened to economic exploitation". He was aghast at the velocity of communication and information exchange and at the incongruity of radio news and entertainment. Instead of enjoying a life rooted in ancestral homes or local cities, modern citizens were bombarded by international trivia. Having lost touch with the earth and history, time had "ceased to be anything but velocity, instantaneousness, and simultaneity". Having summed up the malaise of the age (he wasn't being pessimistic, he insisted), he was back to Being again.

But his problem wasn't with technology *per se*. Instead, he was worried by what he called the "essence of technology": a kind of relentless, aggressive, systematic ordering for its own sake. Heidegger called this a "standing reserve" – like planes on a runway, chocolate bars in a supermarket, or workers in a factory, it's a logic of pure availability. This doesn't mean there aren't winners and losers, but that the logic of technology is beyond political systems and economic imperatives. In fact, it's pure Ananke: an unyielding necessity, indifferent to matters of good and bad, right and wrong. For the Freiburg professor, this was the way in which we "reveal Being" – in other words, what it means to exist at all. Like Marcuse (his student), Heidegger argued that the essence of technology is our modern philosophy of life.

Though very much a child of the modern era (as all Romantics are), Heidegger looked back longingly to an agrarian Arcadia, replete with rustic peasants with calloused hands and heavy bread. Inspired by Van Gogh's painting *A Pair of Shoes*, he once wrote lovingly of peasant boots, "pervaded by uncomplaining worry as to the certainty of bread". Where we might see just dirty old footwear, Heidegger saw "the wordless joy of having once more withstood want ... and shivering at the surrounding menace of death". Something of a rustic dandy (somewhere between Oscar Wilde and the fictional scarecrow Worzel Gummidge), Heidegger would sometimes deliver his lectures in what one biographer called "glorified scouting garb": knickerbockers and a woollen suit. His *Being and Time* was rich with references to old manual tools like hammers and axes and to the humble rural chores of chopping wood. His poetry was a curious mix of idyll and analysis, from cowbells, "slopes of the mountain valley" and wandering herds, to the "topology of Being". Perhaps something was lost in the translation.

To flee from the velocity of modernity, and to enjoy the topology of Being, Heidegger had a little hut built in Todnauberg, in the Black Forest. Of course, he didn't organize or supervise this himself – the job was left to his wife, Elfride (philosophers' wives are often still part-babysitter, part-foreman today). While Heidegger later rented a room from a local peasant (the chalet was too small and his family were noisy), the cabin was an emblem of his philosophical life. It offered a vision of rustic quiet and beauty, far away from the pressures, human complications and mechanized bedlam of the town. In this light, it was not simply a writer's retreat, but a manifestation of man's kinship with natural splendour. A few years after the hut was built, Heidegger wrote his lover, Hannah Arendt, a letter from Todnauberg. Feeling like a "mountain man", he spoke of the "unsuspected powers" awakened by the solitude of the hut, and the humbling yet invigorating wonder of the unalloyed starry sky. "I need," he wrote to her, "such closeness to nature."

It's easy to take the mickey. But with his chalet, Heidegger left a magnificent vision of what technology can do – a tangible alternative to "pure availability". While clearly built by a means-to-end mentality (or it would've remained a pile of lumber), it exemplified tools put to human ends, rather than the other way around. And more importantly, these ends were not about exploitation at work or in the home but the freeing of Heidegger's creativity. He was given a place of peace, quiet and beauty, which inspired his mind to reflect and gave him the circumstances to do so. "My work-world," he called it. It was also a site for family meals (when he wasn't working), first meetings and interviews: a place where strangers and friends could meet the "mountain man" Heidegger wanted to be. If this was a glib Romantic conceit, it was also a kind of genuine self-development. He was using technology to protect his attention, sharpen his perception, safeguard his reflection. He was reclaiming his psyche from the noise of modern life.

Obviously, Heidegger's hut isn't the be-all and end-all of technological salvation – but it's a clue, in the original sense of the word: a trail to follow up, in case we get lost. It suggests that the real danger is allowing the essence of technology to dominate our lives. In this, Heidegger was sensitive to Marcuse's critique. Our instruments, implements and tools can be used to exploit our labour and repress our spontaneity or they can be tools of resistance and art. They can divide us efficiently by gender, class and race or they can bring us together for conversation, consecration or commemoration. Whenever things are running efficiently and precisely, and with an eye for synchronization and integration, there's opportunity for restraint. If we're confronted with perfect, unalterable mathematical certainty, perhaps we need to look for more flexibility or ambiguity (and this goes for books as much as for information technology). If we're transgressing borders and manipulating time, we might need to reassess our immediate relationships. If we've got the munchies after checking email, maybe we need to rethink our internet use. In each case, what's different is not the tool itself, but the vision of life that guides it. At issue are our most basic assumptions about who and what we are. In this way, the essence of technology isn't cogs or computer chips, it's our way of being, *our* "essence". If this is so, then there's no point trying to flee to Arcadia – we can only liberate technology as we unfetter ourselves.

The call of conscience

The struggle of mankind with technology doesn't resemble the wars of science fiction. Instead, it's more private and personal, and it centres on the seemingly banal and familiar relationships between ordinary individuals and the tools of their life. Even if we have a villain like Ananke to conjure up, the essence of technology doesn't look like Hugo Weaving's "Agent Smith" from *The Matrix*. It's much less melodramatic than our dystopian entertainment, though perhaps more unsettling and uncanny than any Hollywood blockbuster.

Yet science fiction does offer some intriguing departure points for speculation. One of the most chilling images from television is that of the Borg from *Star Trek*. They're a race of cold-blooded machine-men, ruthlessly assimilating civilizations for their technologies, seeking "to perfect themselves". Pale, bloodless beings covered in shiny black synthetic suits, they epitomize the stereotypical dangers of technology. Black robotic monocles cover their eyes, and their hands are often replaced by menacing pincers or drills. In the interests of efficiency, the Borg are permanently networked: plugged into a "hive mind", listening to one another's thoughts day and night. When they assimilate new species, the victims' bodies are invaded by tiny machines that transform them into selfless

Borg "drones". Without free will or conscience, these drones are obediently at the service of the Borg collective. When they die, their parts are recycled, and each drone is simply replaced. Like all machines, they are relentless – as reflected in their chilling catchcry "Resistance is futile". They do not stop to laugh, to weep or to sigh. They aren't male or female, nor do they reproduce sexually. They're cyborgs: uncanny hybrids of cybernetic system and organism.

Though they're obviously a Hollywood caricature, the Borg are a suggestive vision of human reality. Like them, we're already fused with technology, regardless of whether this is ancient or modern, manual or automatic. And we always have been. From the humble crafts of Aristotle's Greece to the mechanical presses that printed Heidegger's *Being and Time* and the keyboard I'm typing on, a varied but continuous chain of technology is in use. In this sense, we can't destroy technology, because we're indissolubly linked with it. We can't define ourselves against machines, because they're part of us. Any rebellious plan for overthrowing the reign of technology is likely to be written, distributed and enacted with all sorts of implements, tools and equipment. Instead of embarking on a quixotic quest to kill the digital giant, we would be better off recognizing our technological dependence. There's a little Borg in all of us. (Too much for my editor, that's for sure.)

But there is one crucial way in which we are *not* the Borg: if we are inextricably linked to technology, we don't have the luxury of a "hive mind". We have the weight of liberty: the opportunity and obligation to craft a life. Heidegger once wrote of the call of "Guilty!" that haunts our moments of boredom or anxiety. He wasn't referring to a God or a jury – the voice is our own: the primal, powerful awareness that we have to "be" *something* rather than *nothing*. For Heidegger, this was the "call of conscience", which shakes us out of trivial distractions, and reminds us of our existential responsibilities. Normally, we flee this call – we seek "the entertaining 'incidentals'," as he put it, "with which busy curiosity keeps providing itself". But if we want emancipation from distraction, we have to listen more carefully. Because if we are the ones who have to live and die (rather than machines), then we have to be decisive about the values that inform, motivate and justify our lives. This is something technology will never do for us.

Reclaiming this enterprise won't be the stuff of science fiction or Luddite romance – it won't mean shooting Borg, or angrily dancing on (rather than with) iPods. To overcome the distractions of the technological age, what's needed is a reaffirmation of our own existence – our "stance on Being", as Heidegger might have put it. If we can't escape technology, we can certainly enforce its limits, and our own. We can defer to the noise of YouTube and cable television, or we can seek moments of quiet attention and reflection. We can accept the stress of 24-hour availability, or we can reclaim our own rhythms. (I can answer the mobile phone, or I can savour Ithaca's salt and cyclamen.) If we're the slaves of technological necessity, we have to forge our *own* necessities. In the name of everyday, ordinary freedom, we must be what machines can never be: the custodians of ourselves.

4. A farewell to arms

> We give the impression of being in retirement, and we are nothing of the kind. For if we are genuine in this, if we have sounded the retreat and really turned away from the surface show, then … nothing will distract us.   (Seneca, Letter LVI)

I keenly remember the first time I was kicked in the head. It was an otherwise forgettable evening in *karate* class. We were sparring in *jiyu kumite*, or "free fighting": no breaks, no points, just fighting with medium contact until the teacher yelled "*yame*" to stop. My opponent was a little older, stronger and more patient than I was. He was also a good tactician, with excellent flexibility and power in his legs. At one point, he kicked my face, but I blocked it. He immediately attacked my face and stomach with punches, which I scrambled to block. I forgot about the leg, but it never left the air – his knee just kept hanging there for a few seconds while he got my attention with his hands. Then *thwack*. His foot whacked me in the side of the temple. I backpedalled for a while, trying to regain my composure. Lucky he wasn't trying to really hurt me – he would have done some damage. We kept fighting until the *sensei* stopped us. As I knelt there sweating and smarting, I realized I had learned a valuable lesson: don't be so preoccupied with obvious threats that you miss the real dangers. This is simple in the abstract, but it's not so easy to remember when you're stressed or your time is limited. Sometimes it takes an injury to remind you: in battle, distraction is an invaluable tool.

This anecdote would be no more than trivia, if martial subterfuge weren't so prominent in civilized life. War is at the heart of modern politics, and nowhere is this demonstrated with more honesty and clarity than in Niccolo Machiavelli's *The Prince*. In this classic treatise on statecraft, the Renaissance Florentine revealed how crucial military know-how was for good statesmanship. Whereas his *Discourses on Livy* discussed the foundation and governance of good republics, *The Prince* concentrated on monarchies. For Machiavelli, the most important thing for a ruler was military expertise. To be diverted from war by "pleasures" was a disaster. "A prince," he wrote, "should have no other object or thought, nor acquire skill in anything, except war, its organization, and its discipline."

But Machiavelli didn't just mean war on the battlefield. In order to capture and keep foreign territories, the prince required a keen sense of strategy and tactics. He had to be vicious with strong enemies, generous with weak neighbours, brutal to traitors in public, and heed his advisors in private. Indeed, for Machiavelli it was a terrible mistake to be distracted from the ministry – princes who surrounded themselves with flatterers were always badly informed, and diverted from their tasks. If destiny were as capricious as men ("ungrateful, fickle, liars and deceivers"), the prince needed all his resources to take it in hand firmly – "fortune is a woman," he advised, "and if she is to be submissive it is necessary to beat and coerce her." (If anyone's asking for a smack here, it's Niccolo.) The idea wasn't simply to wait for fate to deliver a kingdom, or simply to rush headlong into the bloody fray – rule required brutality and cunning, force and foresight.

Machiavelli didn't just address himself to wars between political rivals. The battle was as much with citizens as with other monarchs. And while it was important to be liked by the masses, it was better to be feared than adored. "The bond of love is one which men, wretched creatures that they are," wrote Machiavelli, "break when it is to their advantage to do so; but fear is strengthened by a dread of punishment which is always effective." To inspire terror, the good prince razed towns, beheaded dissidents and destroyed enemies – anything to keep the constituency firmly under his thumb.

But he had to be sneaky about it. For example, if the citizens needed taxes or punishment, it was a minister or public official who did the dirty work, while the prince kept his hands clean. In general terms, Machiavelli's prescription was simple: it's fine to have a façade of goodness and righteousness, but keep the reins of monarchy with deceit and manipulation. "One must know how to colour one's actions," he wrote. "Men are so simple, and so much creatures of circumstance, that the deceiver will always find someone ready to be deceived." Whether it's a sword, a constitution, or a left foot that's being used, the enemy wants our minds elsewhere when the coup strikes. Distraction is a favoured tool of the aggressive leader.

Weapons of mass distraction

At first glance, it might seem like the warning doesn't apply to the modern West. After all, Machiavelli was studying monarchies and oligarchies, not democracies. In a democratic State, there are no tyrants or princes to usurp the constituency; in theory, the citizens govern themselves. But it's important to be clear about precisely what democracy is and how it differs from the disenfranchisement and manipulation featured in *The Prince*.

The most compelling vision of the democratic ideal was provided by the Greek-born political philosopher Cornelius Castoriadis. Castoriadis argued that what made democracy genuine wasn't simple ballots, polls, votes and parliaments. Instead, the key to democracy was the citizenry – people's ability to imagine and re-imagine themselves: "Society," he wrote, "is self-creation." He called this the "radical imaginary". When the Greeks developed the world's first democracy, it was not just a new kind of political administration but an attempt to re-envision and re-imagine what it was to be human. The Athenian *polis*, or political community, was autonomous – its social reality was to be decided not by kings, gods or nature but by its citizens. As a society, they decided on what it meant to be a good man, what was necessary to live a good life, and the kinds of governance and administration required to serve this vision. In their art, drama and philosophy, they invented new ways of thinking, perceiving and feeling the drama of the human condition. These were debated in the assembly by farmers and nobles (where they were "under a moral obligation," writes Castoriadis, "to speak their minds"), and discussed in plays like Euripides' shocking *Medea*. While the Athenians succeeded neither in perfecting their city-state nor in sharing it with women and slaves, Castoriadis rightly saw this as the world's first glimpse of genuine democracy. "Greece is the ... *locus* where democracy and philosophy are created," he wrote, "thus ... it is our own origin."

The chief significance of democratic Athens is what we might call the "classical moment". If only for a generation or two, Athens was home to a unique balance between individual and society, order and spontaneity, aggression and tenderness. While Athenians were indebted to a rich and enduring cultural legacy, they weren't uncritical or devoid of spontaneity. They stood back from their own traditions and rituals and were able to assess them confidently and constructively. Behind this was a discriminating and sensitive attention – a refusal to be distracted by superfluous or shallow concerns. Whether in the assembly, at the theatre or on the street, the citizens of Athens showed a tremendous presence of mind. Debating the finer points of foreign policy or metaphysics, or critically appraising Sophocles, they were sophisticated and engaged. As Aristophanes' works suggest, even their smut was politically urbane and self-aware.

The consequence of this attuned state of mind was a mature self-determination, which coloured individual citizens as much as the city-state. While the Athenians were as flawed as all homo sapiens, they weren't in the thrall of dogma or ancient prejudice, nor were they chasing progressive utopias. In a very impressive way, they achieved a fierce independence: of their minds as well as their city-state. The result wasn't simply legislative or executive innovation: it was citizens who were occupied with the enterprise of their own freedom.

While the democratic "moment" no doubt strikes a chord with many today, contemporary Western democracy isn't classical Athens. Our elections don't constitute the kind of grass-roots politics Castoriadis championed – we cede our suffrage to professionals. These careerists jostle for plumb spots, usually as the figureheads of large, bureaucratic parties and interest groups. While these parties and leaders are supposed to represent our political voices, they're far more beholden to powerbrokers, lobby groups, advocates and businesses than they are to ordinary voters (who lack the wealth, education and connections to effectively govern the machinery of State). Policy is formulated, scrutinized and criticized by specialists and is passed or defeated along party lines (except for the odd "conscience vote", which suggests that consciences are usually superfluous). Most parliamentarians haven't the time or the expertise to read the policies they vote for or against, and their parliamentary debates swing between farcical pre-prepared scripts and spontaneous "yo mama" competitions.

Meanwhile, the mainstream media are owned by large multinational corporations that are interested in placating advertisers and entertaining audiences. In this climate, political dialogue and debate are undertaken by professional "talking heads", who either patronize their audience with platitudes, alienate them with jargon or erect a Machiavellian scoreboard of good and bad tactics (for many journalists, the fight is more important than what is fought for). Most citizens are too busy with work and leisure to worry about politics anyway. In Castoriadis's words, "we are living in a system of *lobbies* and *hobbies*".

Far from being Castoriadis's ideal democracy, contemporary politics is closer to Machiavelli's perpetual war. Behind this is the absence of genuine democratic participation. As society isn't the property of the people (the *res publica*, or "public thing"), it's up for grabs – loot to be fought over by seasoned professionals. The outcome isn't always armed conflict but it is certainly militaristic in its guiding principles. The language of politics is thick with military metaphors. At election time, rivals have "campaigns", where they "battle" for votes. There are "skirmishes" on the front pages of newspapers and "bombardments" in advertising, where politicians are "under fire" for their policies. They have meetings in cabinet or caucus to "marshal the troops", and "traitors" soon "fall on their sword" or "lose their head" – "casualties" of the campaign. In an average day's world headlines and blurbs from the "coalition of the willing", we get: "Brown *battles* to take back the *high ground* ... Chancellor to *attack* Conservative proposals", "State Libs *brawl* over vice-president race", "Chavez in *battle* for South America ... Chavez *launched* another verbal *assault*".

As George Lakoff and Mark Johnson argue in *Metaphors We Live By*, these aren't just fancy literary devices. Metaphors govern our lives by giving us a framework within which to make sense of ourselves and the world. We speak of feeling "up" or "down", even though this is nonsense physically – when we're happy or sad, we're not literally on a ladder or below sea level. These metaphors take one experience and use it to characterize another. And in this, metaphors are one of the most fundamental and essential skills of human cognition and communication. They allow us to broaden our perceptions and thoughts, blending insights from many different times and places – what Lakoff and Johnson call "the power of metaphor to create a reality". But as the "politics as war" metaphor shows, they can also narrow our experience. When politicians and the media are saturating audiences with one metaphor over another, they're actually, in Lakoff's words, "imposing another worldview". And by seeing politics as a battleground, we not only defer to the military professionals (congressmen, senators and parliamentarians) but we also allow their war morality to dominate.

Hence, five centuries after Machiavelli's heyday, distraction is a commonly used political tool. In the battle for political territory, subterfuge is essential. Take the 2003 *"Top Gun"* stunt starring United States President George W. Bush. Instead of holding the press conference in the purpose-built media centre, White House staff chose an aircraft carrier. The President arrived dramatically in a military jet, clad in a khaki flight-suit and surrounded by cheering military personnel. The backdrop to his speech was a large banner reading "Mission Accomplished". "Major combat operations in Iraq have ended," said the President, with his trademark drawl. "In the Battle of Iraq, the United States and our allies have prevailed." The carefully crafted impression was that Mr Bush was an experienced former Air Force soldier, with the battlefield at his fingertips and a victory under his belt. Yet on each of these counts, the stunt was misleading. The President was never a serious soldier (he avoided a Vietnam tour), nor was America winning its "Battle of Iraq". But the stunt served its purpose. Like the showmanship of a good magician, it distracted television viewers from the lies that justified the Iraq invasion and the carnage that followed them.

And the Iraq War was also a monumental diversion – from Bin Laden on the loose in Afghanistan, from the millions of "working poor" and from the dubious Republican election victory of 2000. Once the spin doctors had glossed the invasion with stars and stripes, the war efficiently kept audiences distracted ("All you have to do," said Hermann Goering, "is tell them they are being attacked and denounce the pacifists for lack of patriotism"). As for Hurricane

Katrina, the poor and homeless of New Orleans asked for succour and they got a glitzy press conference.

As this suggests, the whole charade is more like a film than a democratic regime, and this is by no means unique to the United States. "The choice of principal leaders," wrote Castoriadis, "boils down to designating the most 'sellable' personalities." And these media stars are grabs at our attention – red herrings whose charms or idiosyncrasies simplify the imperatives of Realpolitik.

In its electoral propaganda, its tactical gambits, its rigid party corps and its lies of omission and false contrition, modern democracy is less Castoriadis's "radical imaginary" and more a war waged against its citizens. And if we're playing war games, we can expect to be the victims of strategic diversion. "The prince," as Machiavelli said, "must know how ... to be a great liar and deceiver." Substitute "senator" or "minister" for "prince", and you have a maxim for today's political battleground.

The upshot is that mainstream politics doesn't live up to the ideals of the "classical moment". It robs moderns of the opportunity to govern themselves, with all the presence of mind and maturity that this implies. Instead of providing a forum for the enrichment and emancipation of its citizens (let alone the "common good"), it is something of a squabble for territory. This isn't a case of "power corrupts", so much as war degrades – it transforms political professionals into cynical generals or obedient troops. Either way, the possibility of genuine self-governance and autonomy is diminished. And the degeneration is exacerbated for the great mass of disenfranchised citizens. Despite the many rights and liberties enshrined in constitutional law or precedent, freedom is curtailed. Deprived of the expertise and opportunity to participate in government, they're left watching from the sidelines ("non-neutral observers"). Whether we are listening to doublespeak sound bites or pundits' score counting, our attention is diverted from the vital decisions that shape nations and their citizens. Even when we are passionately concerned about issues of State, we are rewarded with little or none of the emancipation promised by genuine democracy. As long as war morality dominates the polity, its weapons of mass distraction will endanger our liberty. The task is to achieve a genuine freedom despite these limitations – but how?

The emancipation of Lucius Seneca

To my mind, a striking possibility comes from ancient Rome. Machiavelli often used Rome as the model of good governance – not because it was noble or high-minded but because it knew how to rule. The strongest Roman sovereigns crushed threatening enemies, appeased weak ones, flattered and entertained the masses and killed disloyal senators. It was ugly and brutal, but it worked – for a while, at least. In this legacy, Rome gives a vivid (and often depressing) picture of the degeneration of politics into abject violence and subterfuge. But in the lives of some of its most eminent citizens, it also offers alternatives: possibilities for freedom in the face of martial morality and its tactical distractions.

One fine example is that of Seneca. If Rome were politics at its most ignoble, he was Rome at its most civilized. He was a deeply flawed and tragically unlucky man, but his life was a lasting model of patience, diligence and dignity amid the absurdities of Roman Realpolitik. While eventually a victim of the State, Seneca achieved genuine self-determination within the constraints of his age. He forsook the tactics and trappings of empire for something less grandiose but more ambitious: a politics of character, with freedom as its goal.

Lucius Annaeus Seneca was born in the Roman province of Corduba in Spain (today's Cordova), around the time of Jesus's birth. But while Christ was a lowly Jewish carpenter in an occupied province, Seneca was an equestrian: a rich aristocratic "knight", with family ties to money and power (in one story, his brother Gallio was the governor asked by Corinthian Jews to try Saint Paul). In Rome, Seneca was given a good education in rhetoric, natural science and philosophy, and he soon made a name for himself as a gifted writer, speaker and thinker. After a brief convalescence in Egypt, Seneca was a well-known advocate, senator and author. He spent his days pleading for clients in court, speaking in the senate and writing plays and essays for literate Rome.

Yet it wasn't his legal career that cemented his lasting reputation – it was his political and ethical life. Having endured exile on Corsica for almost a decade (while there, losing his father, brother and wife), Seneca was recalled to Rome by Agrippina: sister of the emperor Caligula, wife and niece of the emperor Claudius and mother of Nero. Agrippina was a strong, intelligent and proud woman, described by the biographer Seutonius as "intriguing, violent, imperious, and ready to sacrifice every principle of virtue, in the pursuit of supreme power or sensual gratification". She wanted Seneca as a tutor to Nero, who would soon be emperor but was dissipated, spoiled and possibly a little mad ("inherent wickedness," said Seutonius). Together with Nero's co-tutor Burrus, an able military man, Seneca took on the greatest professional role of his career: chief minister of Rome (in fact if not in law). It was a fruitful triumvirate. Nero took care of the debauchery and violence while his older tutors ran Rome. Although accused of being a rich, hypocritical womanizer and a "successful upstart", Seneca clearly had a gift for politics and the prudence to apply his talent in a less-than-perfect political landscape.

But in the long term Seneca was rewarded with betrayal. As Nero grew older, he became more debauched, paranoid and cruel. For his family's safety, and like a good Stoic, Seneca gave up his riches and retired to the country. ("The time now spent on gardens and mansions," he told Nero, "shall be devoted to the mind.") But Nero's lackeys and hangers-on had it in for the old philosopher. They stirred up jealousy and envy in the emperor, slandering the Spaniard for casting a shadow on Nero's "literary talent". Eventually, the emperor ordered his death. If Seneca didn't always live like a philosopher, he died like one. Together with his second wife Pompeia, he calmly slit his wrists. When the blood didn't flow fast enough, he also cut open his ankles and the backs of his knees. But the old ascetic was feeble-hearted and his circulation was poor. As he slowly bled, he summoned a secretary and dictated a small dissertation. Like his predecessor Socrates, he then drank hemlock, but it was too late for it to work. After what Tacitus called a "slow and lingering" agony, Seneca was asphyxiated in a vapour bath. He was almost seventy.

What is immediately impressive about Seneca's life and death is his consistent realism – he wasn't a victim of Romantic folly or egotism. While clearly motivated by high ideals, he knew his limitations and those of the State. In an empire plagued by the politics of whimsy and avarice, good men had few bona fide choices. Seneca realized this and did what he could. "A man ... should benefit his fellow men," he wrote, "many if he can, if not, a few; if not a few, those who are nearest; if not these, himself." In the face of intractable empire, this is reasonable advice from an old statesman. If we're short of days, tired or ill, it's pointless to waste our time and vigour on dead-ends. Being civil-minded, Seneca was more than happy to work in the public service (he preferred "a just king" above all). But he recognized that Realpolitik was draining his hours and endangering his family. His counsel was to avoid these distractions. As he put it to his friend Lucilius, "retire into yourself as much as you can".

But Seneca wasn't advocating surrender or a retreat from engagement with the world. A private life away from the wars of State isn't necessarily any happier, healthier or more fruitful. "The fact that a person is living for nobody," wrote Seneca in his last year, "does not automatically mean that he is living for himself." Disavowing mainstream politics as futile and self-serving does not necessarily mean embracing freedom. It's not enough to simply retreat, or to seek the asylum of self-interest. For Seneca, the first necessity was free time, or what the Romans called "*otium*". But the next obligation was to avoid wasting it. In his sparkling little essay "On the Shortness of Life", Seneca lambasted those who whined about mortality while frittering away their days. For him, there was plenty of time to achieve anything a good man might long for. All a happy and long life needed was clarity, diligence and intelligence – to be clear about what we want and firm and straightforward in getting it. Instead of rushing from one pleasure or obsession to another, the wise man calmly follows his plans and goals, and he dismisses all the temptations and annoyances of the transient world ("a plant that is frequently moved," he wrote to a friend, "never grows strong"). For Seneca, *otium* allowed a kind of self-determination – a way to resist the exigencies of domesticity and public life.

And the point of free time was to ask the central question of life: How should we live? As Seneca saw it, the only way to address this properly was philosophy. In his letter XVI to Lucilius, he wrote:

> Philosophy is not an occupation of a popular nature, nor is it pursued for the sake of self-advertisement. Its concern is not with words, but with facts. It is not carried on with the object of passing the day in an entertaining sort of way and taking the boredom out of leisure. It moulds and builds the personality, orders one's life, regulates one's conduct, shows what one should do and what one should leave undone, sits at the helm and keeps one on a correct course as one is tossed about in perilous seas.

Put simply, philosophy was what good men did with their *otium*. While it might seem like an airy entertainment or abstract hobby, philosophy was the finest way to make the most out of life. "Who can doubt," he asked rhetorically, "that life is the gift of the immortal gods, but that living well is the gift of philosophy?" While the liberal arts often turned men into "pedantic, irritating, tactless, self-satisfied bores" (how things have changed), true philosophy illuminated nature, politics and ethics and was practical. It was also a deed, of sorts. In Seneca's eyes, it wasn't self-indulgent pedantry to spend his days reading and writing – it was an act of generosity and largesse. The philosopher synthesized the greatest ideas and insights of the past into his practices and left his own to the future.

Of course, the old man wasn't always so dignified. In a moment of conceit, he wrote to his friend: "this I promise you, Lucilius. I shall find favour among later generations; I can take with me names that will endure as long as mine" (try this on next year's Christmas cards).

Vanity notwithstanding, Seneca's idea was that the buzz and hum of professional life in general, and politics in particular, were dangerous. They distracted men from philosophy, robbing them of the chance to live well. Philosophers like Zeno, Pythagoras and Aristotle might have been arrogant and a little out of touch with everyday proles but they weren't destructive or threatening. "All will teach you how to die," wrote the weary Spaniard, auguring Nero's depravity, "no one of these will force you to die."

As Seneca's courageous death suggests, such a scholarly outlook resulted in a robust practical philosophy. Instead of being shaped and guided by random fortune or the whimsy of politics (which amount to the same thing for a Stoic), the old Roman carefully cultivated his character. From adulthood to death, this enterprise began with a choice: be distracted by life's legion of random accidents and inexorable necessities, or place attention firmly and doggedly on one's own failings, weaknesses and omissions. "What really ruins our characters," said Seneca, "is the fact that none of us looks back over his life." He wrote about his days in letters and constantly reflected on his shortcomings and disappointments. He put himself through tests of his willpower and resilience, like visiting the Saturnalia festival even though he abhorred the drunkenness and profligacy – "remaining dry and sober takes a good deal more strength of will when everyone about one is puking drunk." He read good books, careful not to become distracted by too many ("restlessness ... is symptomatic of a sick mind") – he noted reminders, warnings, suggestions and other helpful passages, using the insights of distant comrades to perfect himself. In writing his own essays and letters, he moulded these into ideal yet practical guides to life. He presented his self to friends as an ideal model, and allowed them to do the same for him – "we should live as if we were in public view," he counselled, "as if someone could peer into the inmost recesses of our hearts."

Imagining himself surveilled, he carefully accounted for his ailments, including asthma, and meditated on his death. "Dying is also one of life's duties," he wrote to Lucilius. In facing his mortality, he wasn't being morbid or self-indulgent; he was being honest about his end and hoping to fortify himself against fear and cowardice. And as we've seen, he died bravely – like a Stoic. In contrast with the self-serving sycophants in Rome, or the alienated proletariat distracted by free games, this was true liberty.

Like all social and political philosophies, Seneca's Stoicism had its shortcomings. Missing from its theory was a concern for the cultivation of sentiment or passion. Obviously, Seneca himself was a man of keen sympathy and intense feeling. His letters were sensitive and thoughtful, and his conduct with Nero demonstrated a familiarity with the emotional foibles of men. But Stoicism was always a philosophy of cognition, not intuition. Men like Seneca were taught (and instructed themselves) to restrain their feelings with rational habits, which harnessed an iron will to a disciplined mind. They give the impression of failed psychoanalytic patients, desperately stuffing down their inclinations and emotions – a kind of training in high-minded repression.

The danger in the cognitive approach isn't so much that it doesn't work, so much as that it does – and the result is noble souls who are lopsided and crooked. They gain mastery over their feelings, but these remain uncultivated and unsophisticated. They lose an appreciation of richer or more subtle sentiments and become pedantic or insensitive (like Seneca's theories of art, as clumsy as his other observations were elegant). Seneca avoided much of this, and perhaps he was lucky. He could still be moved by a moody forest and sing the praises of sublime nature. But then again, Seneca never was a pure Stoic – he was too ambitious, gregarious and pragmatic to live entirely by the tenets of philosophical abstraction. He was a fine man, and a great Roman, before he was a good Stoic. But in his workable Stoicism, we see can an attentive and robust pursuit of freedom, reminiscent of the "classical moment".

But how might this help us today? Something of a neo-Stoic, the French philosopher Michel Foucault devoted considerable attention to this kind of political and ethical practice, which he called the "care of the self". For Foucault, all Seneca's letters, reflections, notes and tests were implements used in this care, or "technologies of the self". They were ways to reclaim and reconsecrate individuality, personality, character, by refusing the tyranny of fate and fickle men. By assessing their habits and inclinations, and judiciously reining in their proclivities with reason, the Stoics were shaping themselves anew. "Freedom," Foucault told an interviewer in 1984, "has a political model insofar as being free means not being a slave to oneself and one's appetites." Foucault's endeavour required not only clear analysis of what was repressive or restricting but also the cultivation of new practices, rituals, restraints. It involved "a certain relationship of domination, of mastery" over oneself. Mastery was at work in eating, drinking, friendship and sexuality, helping the Stoics to escape the traps of addiction, distraction and unthinking obedience. For Foucault, the care of the self enabled a life of self-direction and self-sufficiency – the "technologies of the self" were tools for freedom.

As Foucault saw it, the project of self-mastery was increasingly relevant to today's political climate. He recognized that politicians weren't ruling citizens in any traditional sense – there's no Nero in the modern West. But for Foucault, this didn't mean there wasn't a dire need for emancipation. On the contrary, it was more vital than ever. One of his chief contributions to knowledge was his theory of "governmentality". Basically, he argued that the rights and liberties of modern capitalist democracy were deceiving. They afforded an enormous amount of individual freedom, but they also went hand in hand with precise and often devious forms of control. For Foucault, we weren't simply oppressed by aberrant coercion or violence – instead, we were rendered obedient by the very institutions of civilized life. The church, schools, prisons, the military and medicine all made claims on our lives, seeking to impose a very specific idea of humanity on our bodies and minds. They rewarded and punished, censured and promoted, and were gatekeepers of authority and privilege. And all this was achieved with an aura of consecrated truth. In this way, the technologies of the self were deployed, but they remained instruments of docility rather than of freedom. Foucault's crucial insight wasn't simply that people were influenced or manipulated but that they became who and what they are at the hands of others. More disturbingly, the tools for doing so were becoming ever more precise and ubiquitous. At work, employees slowly adapted to timesheets, corporate protocols and new forms of telecommunications. At home, they adjusted to new rhythms of entertainment, leisure, transport and domesticity. For Foucault, the average citizen wasn't simply harassed and bullied by the authorities – they were shaped as loyal workers and consumers, in an uncompromising and unquestioned capitalist worldview. And this is why Foucault turned to Stoicism, early Christianity and the classical care of the self. These offered a model of political enfranchisement, reclaiming the critical urge to fashion character and the skills to do so.

Importantly, Foucault was not apolitical, retreating from a brutal world into high theory. He was keenly interested in the machinations of the day, speaking eloquently on issues from Iranian revolution to social security and to Marxism in France and abroad. He was once a member of the French Communist Party and a friend of the French Minister for Justice, and he took part in a violent occupation of the University of Paris VIII (throwing rocks at police in his black velour suit). But his political affiliations and demonstrations, like his sexual experimentations, weren't blueprints or ideal models. He spoke of them as "limit-experiences", encounters that were transformative in their difference, opposition, marginality and intensity. A similar mood of personal change is found in his writings. In a famous interview with an Italian journalist, he spoke of his books as "invitations ... public gestures". They didn't provide a plan of action – they afforded readers a very particular way of perceiving, feeling and thinking. What the audience chose to do with this was their own responsibility. For Foucault, it wasn't the place of the intellectual to tell everyone how to live (an abyss separates this from Plato's philosopher-kings, but also from self-righteous shock-jocks and self-help gurus). Instead, he wanted to "shut the mouths" of vociferous problem-solvers and moral authorities.

Like Seneca's "retirement", the significance of Foucault's position lies in its resistance to both battleground politics and the paralysing cynicism it can breed. In an interview given in the last year of his all-too-brief life, Foucault admitted that he'd "not got very far" in thinking about a contemporary care of the self. But his care of the self was a genuine political engagement – it simply rejected dogmatism and easy answers. Even as HIV/AIDS ravaged his body, Foucault didn't seem frozen by dismay or disappointment; he wasn't a bitter radical, facing mortality with a sense of regret or disenchantment. "If I don't ever say what must be done," he said, "it isn't because I believe there's nothing to be done; on the contrary, it is because I think there are a thousand things to do, to invent, to forge, on the part of those who ... have decided to resist or escape." If we are to discover ways out of bondage or weakness, the discovery is itself part and parcel of the liberation. Like Seneca, Foucault sought freedom in the unique synthesis of character. And in his last years he was hopeful for this very reason: we might yet forsake the subterfuge of mainstream politicking for the existential struggle.

Monstrous liberty

The turn to the self represents a genuine attempt to develop freedom in opposition to mainstream politicking. But to resist the demands and distractions of State and market, it's important to be clear about what this liberty isn't. Most crucially, it's not simply belligerence, recalcitrance or egoism. If emancipation is conflated with the sovereignty of some perfect, authentic "I", it actually becomes a kind of enslavement. The "liberated" remain in the thrall of their unchecked anxieties and fantasies, obeying impulse and idiosyncrasy as if they were divine laws. And in this condition, the tactics of Machiavellian statecraft are actually more potent – lacking self-awareness and self-control, conservatives and radicals alike blunder around blindly in the fog of war.

A telling example of misguided freedom is the Russian revolutionary Mikhail Bakunin. By the end of his life, Bakunin hated states and empires as much as he cherished freedom. "I am a fanatical lover of liberty," wrote Bakunin in 1870, "considering it ... the unique condition under which intelligence, dignity and human happiness can develop and grow." To fight for this vision of human dignity, Bakunin eventually became an anarchist.

Nowadays, the word *anarchy* is often used pejoratively, to mean disorder, chaos, mayhem – to be an "anarchist" is to be a professional bedlam-chaser. But in ancient Greek, *anarchia* simply means "no rulers": no king, no aristocracy, no professional politicians. If monarchy and oligarchy are the governance of the one or the few, anarchism is self-governance: genuine liberty for individuals, without the State interfering in their affairs. This didn't mean rejecting society or community – as Bakunin wrote, "a radical revolt by man against society would … be just as impossible as a revolt against Nature". Society, for Bakunin, was the natural birthplace of individuals; community was the condition for man's self-development.

By contrast, Bakunin believed that states were a curious blend of nature and culture: all the viciousness of the jungle, but in a formal, abstract and mechanized form. They were as aggressive to their own citizens as they were to each other. In other words, they exemplified Machiavellian politics: their fundamental existence was prefaced on violence and deceit. While thinkers like Hobbes and Locke spoke of the State as a "social contract", Bakunin called this "an absurd fiction, and what is more, a wicked fiction". He never signed away his liberty to Russia, nor did any other man, woman, or child – states claimed citizens as their own, then shackled them with laws and punishments. States gave themselves the right to kill and maim in war and prisons, while keeping their citizens at bay with their laws. They would shoot or hang their own subjects, or torture them in prisons. "The great and powerful states could be founded and maintained only by crime," Bakunin wrote, "by many great crimes – and by a thorough contempt for anything called honesty." The states put men to work, and sent them to war, and Bakunin wanted to liberate them from both. Like the older Seneca, his care of the self, his liberty, was a withdrawal from all that smacked of party politics and statesmanship. And this is what often terrified statesmen and infuriated Marx. Whether it was the French Republic, the British Commonwealth, or Marx's "dictatorship of the proletariat", Bakunin wanted it destroyed.

Over the past two-hundred years, anarchists have tried to keep Bakunin's project alive. In the Paris Commune, anarchists fought and worked alongside Jacobins and workers as they lauded Bakunin's writings (while circumspect, Bakunin called the Commune "a bold, clearly formulated negation of the State"). Anarchists fought against Fascists in Spain, where they earned the praise of George Orwell for their courage, loyalty and candour. "Something in his face deeply moved me," he wrote of an Italian militiaman in *Homage to Catalonia*. "It was the face of a man who would commit murder and throw away his life for a friend." Strikes, sit-ins, occupations and rebellions all over Europe were launched by anarchists, or those they've influenced (like the autonomous Marxists). In Europe, the United States and Australia, many anarchists are involved in the Antifa movement, fighting neo-Nazi gangs' intimidation and violence. In the spirit that moved Orwell, some have lost their lives in clashes with white supremacists. In Latin America anarchists are working with grass-roots activists and community groups on everything from radio shows to schools for the poor (which also exist in rural and working-class areas in the West). Mexican anarchists have used non-violent means to defend communes from police, while young Australian anarchists known as the "Arterial Block" fought police during the G20 meetings. ("At times the Paris end of Collins Street," wrote one newspaper, "looked more like Paris '68.") Activists and commentators like Noam Chomsky and Germaine Greer are identified with anarchism, as was the late French photographer Henri Cartier-Bresson ("Long live Bakunin!" he cried in interviews). As an ardent agitator in many of these countries, and journalist of the cause, Bakunin is alive in the minds of many freedom lovers.

But if his name still resounds for throngs of anti-capitalist activists and malcontents, the giant Russian actually achieved very little in his all-too-short life. He was an inspiration for his comrades and their later successors, but his name is barely heard nowadays. Next to the lavish bequest of Marx, for example, Bakunin's legacy is a weak one. In the twentieth century, rebels flying Marx's banner took control of Russia, China, Cuba, North Korea and Vietnam, and communist guerrillas and militia have threatened governments the world over. For many during the Cold War, the "reds under the bed" were a genuine peril, while the moon landing was seen as a slap in the face for Marxist–Leninist Russia (the Americans' Germans were better than the Soviets' Germans). All in all, Bakunin's dreams of a great libertarian socialist revolution were in vain – the last two centuries belong to the Marxists and the bourgeoisie.

And their victory extends to the realm of ideas. While Bakunin has a great many essays and journalistic articles, they are piecemeal and often compromised with heavy-handed rhetoric. As his biographer E. H. Carr wrote, "few men whose life and thought have exercised so powerful an influence on the world as those of Michael Bakunin have left so confused and imperfect a record of their opinions." By contrast, Marx has a massive and well-documented oeuvre. Despite his own penchant for diversionary polemics, his three-volume *Das Kapital* is a whopping great work, testament to its author's intelligence, education and tenacity (even if edited by Engels). All around the world he is lauded as a philosopher and political thinker; he is the subject of countless books, journal articles, theses and essays. And it's not just the boffins: in a British poll, Marx was recently voted the "greatest thinker of the millennium" (Einstein was runner-up). Bakunin didn't rate a mention.

There are many reasons for Bakunin's obscurity, but a crucial one was his lifelong inability to focus; to concentrate his attention and energy on what he wanted and how to achieve it. At Artillery School as a teen, he was distracted by pretty young women. But his dalliances were never consummated, because he was diverted from amorous love by idealism (yet another virgin philosopher, along with his boyhood idol Kant). While he was an impassioned student, his studies of Hegel were unfinished, as were so many of his intellectual endeavours – while a gifted thinker, he remained incoherent and self-contradictory as a scholar.

Bakunin's revolutionary schemes also lacked sober attention. When he was in Dresden, he completely missed the burgeoning opportunity for rebellion – he was plotting for distant (and fanciful) Bohemian uprisings when Richard Wagner (who wrote of Bakunin's "primitive exuberance and strength") bumped into him on the street and dragged him to the town hall. Instead of patiently developing a plan for revolution – as Marx was doing at the same time – the great Russian launched himself into every half-baked plot, wasting his own faculties and everyone else's money (he squandered cash like a true aristocrat). He founded all sorts of secret societies, alliances and brotherhoods, complete with codes, passwords and invisible ink (like a Boy's Own adventure, except with beards). But many of these seemingly dangerous sects never actually existed – they were the products of Mikhail's buzzing brain.

Bakunin's fanciful approach came to a head later in Bakunin's life, when he eagerly followed up the most unlikely sources of revolt. When he met the cankered pseudo-revolutionary Sergei Nechaev, the young Russian fired Bakunin's imagination with tales of rebellion, introducing him to his "Russian revolutionary committee". But it turned out that Nechaev's "committee" was a lie – he was, as E. H. Carr puts it, "a fanatic, swashbuckler, and cad" but not a genuine insurgent leader. Hilariously, Bakunin then enrolled Nechaev in his "World Revolutionary Alliance", which he had just invented. The situation was tragically comic, with two self-styled world-shakers joining one another's imaginary cadres – as if two naked emperors had eagerly agreed to swap their clothes. When Bakunin joined the International in 1868, he had already lost years to ill-fated plots (sailing to Poland with a band of mercenaries – they got as far as Sweden) and the dead-end causes of radical nationalism and pan-Slavic rebellion.

For most of his life, Bakunin displayed a weakness for impulses that stopped him from thinking clearly and acting thoughtfully. As a young man, Bakunin's symptoms were recorded by the writer Vissarion Belinsky: "Strength, undisciplined power, unquiet, excitable, deep-seated spiritual unrest, incessant striving for some distant goal, dissatisfaction with the present". And they were chronic – he drank, ate and smoked to excess (when he could), feverishly eating large spoonfuls of sardines, or spending "revolutionary" francs on a cigar. "Bakunin has become a monster," wrote Marx to Engels in 1863, "a huge mass of flesh and fat." It was as if the fulfilment of Bakunin's political program was indistinguishable from the immediate and excessive satisfaction of his basest urges. Even in his last years, he threw away a fortune (not his own, of course) on a soon to be barren Swiss estate and told his wife, Antonia, that his inheritance had paid for it. When it all went pear-shaped, the obese, toothless Goliath hurled himself into an abortive Italian coup to hide his shame. Within two years he was dead, his huge coffin the laughing-stock of local grave-diggers.

It is convenient to blame Bakunin's failures on his idealistic opposition to capitalism or modern forms of governance. But to my mind, his problem wasn't his taste for emancipation or his anarchism (which can be a potent practical philosophy). More than many like-minded scholars and rebels, he had a keen nose for liberty and its attendant passions. He was, as he himself put it, "a fanatical lover of liberty". His chief failing was to mistake this raw urge for the enterprise of freedom itself. And in this state of nascent maturity, he stumbled myopically from disaster to disaster. Rather than rejecting the military machinations of State, he aped them. Rather than capitalizing on opportunities, he wasted or ignored them. Put simply, Bakunin gave so much attention to his illusory schemes and fantastic enemies, he never properly concentrated on himself; on the qualities of personality that would have genuinely emancipated him. As a result, he never embodied the freedom he so adored.

Nevertheless, the more I read about Bakunin, the more I liked him. Perhaps it's the Romantic in me, or perhaps it's just a fondness for loveable rogues. Apart from my appreciation of his ideas on the State and capitalism, I admired his warped character. I was swept up in his tireless enthusiasm, charisma and appetite for food, friendship and art. It was like watching the adventures of a hairier, Slavic Byron, complete with capricious intimate relations and bungled military campaigns. There's something very seductive about this unleashing of impulse and idiosyncrasy. Perhaps like Bakunin, many of us have dreamed of smashing the engines of State or inflicting all sorts of Dantesque punishments on fickle politicians (making them watch their own election advertisements for eternity, for example). Confronted by the violence of nations and chicanery of corporations, it's reasonable to either retreat into privative egoism or fantasize about glorious revolution.

But as the tragedy of the "toothless giant" suggests, these reactions lead to very much the same thing: monstrous liberty, marked by the degeneration of character, and the transformation of liberty into juvenile self-assertion. For these reasons, an alternative to the politics of distraction will be found not in unruly Romanticism but in the cultivation of clarity, honesty and strength. It's exemplified not by Bakunin's wayward anarchism but in the classical discipline of Seneca and Foucault. Genuine freedom requires not only a struggle against authority but also a more attuned and discerning engagement with ourselves.

Adventures in liberty

There is a helpful idea that encapsulates this – an idea with history. When Alfred North Whitehead coined the phrase "adventures of ideas", he hit upon an illustrative metaphor. There's something exciting, something exploratory, about the way thoughts travel. They are born in one country, among an idiosyncratic mix of popular opinion and politics, and they soon shrivel and die. They disappear for generations, only to live again on foreign soil, in a new ensemble of aspirations and anxieties. "There will be," wrote

Whitehead, "a general idea in the background flittingly, waveringly – or perhaps never expressed in any adequate universal form with persuasive force." The idea of the soul, for example, was important to the Greeks, but waned as a motivating notion. But in the minds of Christians it achieved a new grandeur. Wedded to the earnest fragility of the new Christian outlook, it remained in the European consciousness for thousands of years. As Whitehead put it, "it is a hidden driving force, haunting humanity, and ever appearing in specialised guise".

Another such idea, and one that colours my vision of freedom, is *Bildung*. Popularized by the great German philosopher, linguist and statesman Wilhelm von Humboldt, *Bildung* means "self-realization", "self-development" "or self-culture". As the latter suggests, *Bildung* requires culture to exist and succeed. For Humboldt, one of the central aspects of culture was language. He proposed that the languages of cultures were tightly interwoven with their thoughts, perceptions and emotions. In the past, philosophers had seen words only as abstract signs – mental copies of, or labels for, things in the world. They were simply tools for individuals, while national languages were just toolsets. For Humboldt, however, language was a living activity, essential to the unique principles and rituals of cultures. To speak German was to partake in a world different from that of the Native Indian or the urbane Frenchman. Humboldt was here carrying on the work of Romantics like Herder and Hamann. Instead of atomistic individuals competing for glory or cash, this was a theory of community, what the German sociologists Ferdinand Tönnies and Weber called *Gemeinschaft*: the kind of close-knit, communal ties lauded by Romantic nationalists.

But in Humboldt's version of *Bildung*, the community never became a Romantic caricature: a Fascist authoritarian "we" or the enemy of the capricious but authentic "I" (like that of Bakunin). Instead, the ideal was a free and enlightened engagement with past and present culture, and an endeavour to incorporate their achievements into life. While "culture" can have snobby or hipster connotations ("When I hear the word culture," wrote artist Barbara Kruger with irony, "I take out my chequebook"), Humboldt's vision was both more sober and more ambitious. The purpose and reward of *Bildung* was neither glory nor happiness but the perfection of character. As Humboldt put it, "the development of all the germs that are present in the individual conformation of human life, this is what I consider the true goal of man on earth, not precisely happiness." In other words, our ultimate duty is not to be happy but to be free: to perfect our individuality by forging ourselves with the aid of our cultural inheritance.

Humboldt's striking vision of *Bildung* influenced a generation of German scholars, students and statesmen. As the Prussian Minister of Education, he was one of the founders of the liberal University of Berlin, now Humboldt University. His portrait of university education was a unity of teaching and research, facts and imagination, freedom and public service. In an atmosphere of "freedom and the absence of distraction", academics were to collaborate with students and with one another. The ideal was a "ceaseless effort" of cultivation and edification, where the free individuality of each student and staff member led to a brimming ferment of thought, perception and emotion. While state politics and human failings meant universities always fell short of this, Humboldt's ideal was stirring. It left German scholars with a rich legacy of self-culture and inspired educators and reformers in America and England.

One such leader was the well-known English philosopher, politician and state official John Stuart Mill (Bakunin read his autobiography, as did Nietzsche). Mill's very successful *On Liberty* was epigraphed with a Humboldt quote, and in his biography Mill wrote of the German scholar's "unqualified championship" of liberty and individualism. In Mill, the ideas of Herder and Hamann continued their wayward adventure into nineteenth-century England. Via Humboldt's keen love of freedom and self-determination, enlightened German Romanticism lived on in Britain's greatest public philosopher.

Mill's life and work deserve close attention because they offer an alternative to the somewhat cerebral philosophy of Stoicism and the bungling self-aggrandizement of Bakunin. In a very tangible way, Mill's career suggests how genuine liberty is an ongoing cultural achievement rather than a simple matter of cynical statecraft or privative egotism. Reminiscent of Seneca's worldly pragmatism, it demonstrates how freedom can be sought in an honest, passionate, patient politics of character.

As a young boy, Mill appeared the epitome of Humboldt's *Bildung*. His father, the Scottish polymath James Mill, gave the lad an extensive training in history, languages and philosophy. From the ages of eight to ten, Mill read many of the world's finest works of Greek and Latin literature, and translated passages into English (he began his Greek studies at the age of three, and Latin at the ripe old age of eight). In typical nineteenth-century style, John Stuart's father would take him on walks where they would discuss the boy's readings and comprehension. "With my earliest recollections of green fields and wild flowers," wrote Mill, "is mingled that of the account I gave him daily of what I had read the day before." *Don Quixote* and *Arabian Nights* were allowed sparingly as "books of amusement" (James had to borrow them for his son). Before puberty, young John Stuart had read more of the West's classics, in their original tongues, than many of today's postgraduate students. And for his "private reading", he read William Mitford's *History of Greece*, Hooke and Ferguson's Roman histories, while "flattering himself" by writing a history of Roman government (which he destroyed as an embarrassed young man). When young Mill was thirteen, his father put him through "a complete course of political economy", supplemented by lessons from James's friend, the renowned economist David Ricardo.

And for his son's edification, James added moral lessons to those of the liberal arts and natural sciences. While highly intelligent and educated, John Stuart wasn't to be proud or conceited, or puff himself up next to his slower peers. He was to measure himself not against other children, or against the common English gentleman, but against the ideal of man – what mattered was "not what other people did," wrote John Stuart years later, "but what a man could and ought to do." Here again is Humboldt's *Bildung*, nascent but influential in Mill's English upbringing. Instead of deferring to the status quo or leaving character to Fate, Mill was given the skills to deliberately and discerningly cultivate himself. "Man's true objective," wrote Humboldt two generations before, "prescribed not by his changeable inclination but by his unchangeable reason, is the greatest proportional development of his energies aimed at the construction of a complete whole." For men like Humboldt and James Mill (men of radically differing lives and temperaments), mankind was the child of reason and will, not whimsy, chance or caprice.

As a young man, John Stuart Mill lived up to Humboldt's ideal. His father arranged a steady job for him in the British East India Company, where he worked for over three decades (he was seventeen when he got the post). When he wasn't proofreading or drafting correspondence for India, he was writing letters and articles for newspapers. His mentor Jeremy Bentham established a "radical" utilitarian periodical, the *Westminster Review*, and at the age of today's first-year university students, young Mill wrote more articles than his father, Bentham, or their older peers. Very much his father's son, John Stuart earnestly applied his philosophical ideals to Britain's government and civic society and cultivated his reformer's mind at every chance (sharpening his wit in his "little knot of young men"). "Ambition and desire of distinction, I had in abundance," wrote Mill in his autobiography, "and zeal for what I thought the good of mankind was my strongest sentiment." In the spirit of Humboldt's faith in "unchangeable reason", young John Stuart was level-headed, diligent and logical.

Behind this very British life of patient work, sober speculation and civilized reform was Bentham's utilitarianism. While utilitarianism now comes in many guises (and has serviced many political creeds), Bentham's basic philosophy was quite simple. For Bentham, all the metaphysical systems of Aristotle and Plato were just so much poppycock. All that men can know about right and wrong is what gives pleasure and pain. "Nature," he wrote, "has placed mankind under the governance of two sovereign masters, pain and pleasure. It is for them alone to point out what we ought to do, as well as to determine what we shall do." Though this was first argued by the Hellenistic philosopher Epicurus (whose work Seneca was fond of, despite their rival traditions), Jeremy Bentham modernized and popularized it.

And popular it was, for good reason. In Bentham's "principle of utility", the Britons of the nineteenth century were given a simple and clear way to decide what to do and how to do it. If something was going to increase happiness – what Bentham called "benefit, advantage, pleasure, good" – then they should do it. And this applied to states as much as citizens. The principle of utility recognized no community ("a fictitious body," said Bentham), except the summed interests and happiness of individuals. So ethical living and good national policy were just a matter of cool-headed calculation. But if the currency of this economics of happiness was pleasure and pain, then these had to be valued. To do this, the good utilitarian examined their intensity, duration, certainty and proximity and whether they would cause more pleasure and pain. He then added them all up and checked the balance. If there was happiness at the end of the equation, then the legislation, policy or deed was in the black. The utilitarian doctrine was simply a happiness machine.

But John Stuart Mill wasn't happy. In fact, he was miserable. At the age of twenty, he had everything he had ever wanted. He was progressing in his studies, was writing well-regarded letters and articles, and was surrounded by like-minded, generous and thoughtful men. But he was depressed. He tried sleeping – it did nothing. He read his favourite books, but they left him cold. Quoting Coleridge's poetry, Mill endured what he called a "drowsy, stifled, unimpassioned grief" – a kind of lingering ennui, which drained his mental and physical vitality. "I became persuaded," he wrote, "that my love of mankind, and of excellence for its own sake, had worn itself out." He still wrote his reformist works and his correspondences for the East India Company, but there was no joy, no happiness. Despite all his intelligence and diligence, the very thing Bentham's utilitarianism promised was missing. "I was," he wrote in his autobiography, "left stranded at the commencement of my voyage, with a well-equipped ship and a rudder, but no sail."

Mill's despair dragged on for six long months. He told no one, not even his father, preferring instead to wrestle with his "incubus" privately and quietly. It wasn't until he read the autobiography of the Encyclopedist writer Jean-François Marmontel that he saw the light. In one passage of Marmontel's memoirs, the young man lost his father. In a moment of tragic sweetness, he promised to take his father's place. "Mother, brothers, sisters, we experience ... the greatest of afflictions," said young Marmontel, "let it not overcome us. Children, you lose a father, and you find one; I am he, I will be a father to you; I adopt all his duties; you are no longer orphans." Having read this, after months of lethargy and numbness, John Stuart Mill wept. And when he did, his despair eased. He was once again cheered by books, conversation and sunny days. His philanthropy returned, along with his faith in the patient perfection of character. To preserve his own metaphor, he now had sails for his sturdy liberal boat.

As the younger Mill saw it, there were two reasons for his "mental crisis". The first was Bentham's theory of happiness. As a teenager and young adult, Mill had been captivated by Bentham's philosophy but he admitted that the caricature of a Benthamite as "mere reasoning machine" was right. In place of a rich philosophy of human flourishing, Bentham had calculation and analysis. He misrecognized not only the material and spiritual conditions of happiness (the Romantic notion Bentham dismissed as a "fiction") but also the philosophical methods of acquiring this happiness. And added to Bentham's philosophical shortcomings were James Mill's prejudices. While a spirited and loving man, "in his personal qualities", as John Stuart put it, "the Stoic predominated". So like Seneca, James taught his son an unyielding interrogation of the soul. But whereas the Roman ruthlessly explored his anxieties, fears and desires (and often tried to eradicate them), Mill learned from Bentham to concentrate on happiness. And this single-minded philosophical attention to private "benefit, advantage, pleasure, good" killed his joy. After his depression, he learned that the ideal was to focus not solely on happiness but on good words, thoughts and deeds. Like Marmontel, the crucial thing was to think of others – to make his mission the alleviation of suffering in friends, family, citizens and foreign strangers. "Ask yourself whether you are happy," he wrote, "and you cease to be so. The only chance is to treat, not happiness, but some end external to it, as the purpose of life. Let your self-consciousness, your scrutiny, your self-interrogation, exhaust themselves on that." In short, what we need are noble ambitions, not self-indulgent plans for our own fulfilment.

Nietzsche once famously attacked utilitarianism, quipping: "Man does not strive after happiness; only the Englishman does that". But having conquered his depression, Mill sought precisely Nietzsche's "a Yes, a No, a straight line, a goal". The utilitarian theory of happiness would no longer distract John Stuart from the very things that made him happy.

The second reason for his depression was the overly intellectual character of his training – a failing common to utilitarianism and Stoicism. Both traditions were of a cognitive bent, and tended to downplay the importance of emotion and imagination – no particular love of art, poetry or literature can be found in

Bentham, Seneca or the acolytes of each. The Stoic way was always to suppress, to rein in – to put a stop to the passions with thought and will. And two millennia later, Jeremy Bentham and James Mill were little different. As a student of these men and their schools, John Stuart not only fractured his happiness with analysis, but also failed to tend his stunted feelings.

Mill's ennui evoked a broader, more sympathetic consciousness. "I ... for the first time," he wrote, "gave its proper place, among the necessities of human well-being, to the internal culture of the individual." Instead of turning to Byron's impulsive Romanticism (which Bakunin would have loved) he sought England's pastoral poets. He realized that the poems of Wordsworth, for example, inspired in him a mood of joy. "Thanks to the human heart by which we live," wrote Wordsworth in "Intimations of Immortality", "Thanks to its tenderness, its joys, and fears, / To me the meanest flower that blows can give / Thoughts that do often lie too deep for tears." Lines like these not only evoked the landscapes of Mill's youth but also elegantly wedded cognition to passion and a love of beauty. These fed into his yearning to help mankind with its struggles and imperfections. "In them I seemed to draw," he wrote, "from a source of inward joy, of sympathetic and imaginative pleasure, which could be shared by all human beings." Neglected by Mill's classical and contemporary teachers, the arts were essential to *Bildung*. They revealed and refined his emotions instead of simply repressing them, while they encouraged his sense of human fellowship. In other words, they were an education in the passions of happiness.

Of course, Mill wasn't a revolutionary, in word or deed. He was a dutiful servant of the State as a functionary of the East India Company and liberal parliamentarian. He endorsed the doctrine of "free trade", which has chiefly been light on freedom and heavy on trade. In its nineteenth- and twentieth-century incarnations, the free trade ideology has done precious little to aid the planet's poor and disenfranchised. If anything, it has left them to the whims of multinational corporations and the developing nations who court them. And, like Bentham, Mill's utilitarianism reduced human beings to hedonistic atoms, even if he admitted noble pleasures into his philosophy ("better to be Socrates unsatisfied," wrote Mill famously in *Utilitarianism*, "than a pig satisfied"). Perhaps Mill was guilty of not being quite "German" enough, of being too much the embodiment of his own laissez-faire Britain.

Yet in his life of reflection and legislation, there's hope for us today. Mill's legacy is not just pages of logic and political philosophy but the achievement of a unique modern liberty. While holding down an important and demanding professional appointment, he gave his leisure hours – his *otium*, in Seneca's parlance – to educate himself, aid friends and strangers, and reform his nation. He was rightly cautious of the State, and was happy to admit this. "A State which dwarfs its men," he wrote, "will find that with small men no great thing can be accomplished." Importantly, this wasn't a retreat from political struggle – a puritanical fear of the pollution of pragmatism. Nor was it an attempt to enjoy the benefits of the nation and State without any of the contributions and sacrifices. Despite his concerns, Mill pressed ahead, believing that the cultivation of laws and men were complementary. "Though I am sick of politics," he wrote in one letter, "I do not despair of improvement." At the heart of this was his unflagging endorsement of reason, responsibility and the value of distinctive individuality. The purpose of government was not to repress individuality but to encourage it. He wrote in *On Liberty*:

> It is not by wearing down into uniformity all that is individual in themselves, but by cultivating it ... that human beings become a noble and beautiful object of contemplation; and as the works partake the character of those who do them, by the same process human life becomes rich, diversified, and animating, furnishing more abundant aliment to

high thoughts and elevating feelings, and strengthening the tie which binds every individual to the race, by making the race infinitely better worth belonging to.

In passages like these, Mill showed himself to be a man of his liberal age, but an exemplary one. In an age of religion, he was an atheist; of capitalism, a "qualified socialist" (of the utopian sort); and of institutionalized misogyny, a feminist. And while Nietzsche spoke of Mill as a "flathead", no deadened Benthamite caricature could have written with such sensitivity and penetration about landscape and poetry (which was, he told Thomas Carlyle, "higher than Logic").

In his humble, polite English way (what Nietzsche unfairly called the "spirit of respectable but mediocre Englishmen"), John Stuart Mill grasped the freedom sought by Bakunin and Seneca, but without their idiosyncratic flaws. In his darkest hours of depression, he felt crushed by the relentless Necessity of fact, circumstance and mechanical cause and effect. However, in his epiphany, he realized that the essence of liberty wasn't some grand metaphysical purity above these but the earnest practice of self-culture, self-development. "What is really inspiring and ennobling in the doctrine of freewill," he wrote, "is the conviction that we have real power over the formation of our character." In other words, freedom is the invention and application of our own necessities, from our own crooked timber, and the chaotic flotsam of the world. And this can't happen if we are simply chasing our own happiness (either with Bentham's intellect, or Bakunin's caprice) or neglecting our emotional life. When Stoics or utilitarians shunned the arts, they were injuring their characters no less than Bakunin, feeding his "undisciplined power" with Beethoven's Ninth Symphony. By judiciously engaging with good books, conversations, deeds and artworks, Mill revivified *Bildung*. "Human nature," he said in *On Liberty*, "is not a machine to be built after a model ... but a tree, which requires to grow and develop itself on all sides, according to the tendency of the inward forces which make it a living thing."

With his living ideal of human flourishing, John Stuart avoided the distractions of Machiavellian statecraft and the allure of private egotism. Instead of simply deferring to the status quo, or blindly railing against it, he concentrated on the sustained and many-sided development of his character. He incorporated the finest aspects of his upbringing and schooling, and judiciously jettisoned others. And as a parliamentarian and outspoken intellectual, this enterprise served him well. But his lasting achievement was not his policies or philosophies but himself. His character was both the means to his enduring public life and an end in itself. Of course we can't all be John Stuart Mill, but this isn't the point – he had to *become* what he was, and this is the challenge for everyone disenchanted with the status quo. Over a century since his death, Mill's life remains a unique accomplishment: a political career, ennobled by the confident and untiring cultivation of liberty.

5. Matisse's hernia

> I don't need to make churches; there are other people to do that ... the problem is to create a certain atmosphere, another one there ... something that sublimates, elevates people above the ordinary, the day-to-day.
> (Henri Matisse to Brother Rayssiguier, 15 November 1948)

At first blush, it seems Henri Emile Benoit Matisse was the perfect bourgeois son: intelligent, well educated and a trained lawyer. Working in a provincial notary's office as a clerk in 1890, Matisse was all set for a stable and financially rewarding legal career. But he was bored stiff by law ("it was Hebrew to me"), and only persisted out of pragmatism and loyalty, and for want of anything else to do. He spent his days copying dry legal documents, and when boredom set in he entertained himself by shooting passers-by with putty pellets from a glass peashooter.

This juvenile dissent would be an unremarkable fact in the history of law if it weren't for what followed. Not long into his appointment, the young man was struck with a severe hernia (or something like it – Matisse's diagnoses changed as he aged). Bedridden in hospital, Matisse was unable to work, or even to walk. It was assumed that he would recover, continue his apprenticeship and graduate to a higher office. But radical, life-altering change came from an unlikely quarter. His mother, Anna Héloise, gave him some paints, brushes and canvases, hoping to take his mind off his convalescence. Of course, these tools weren't supposed to be taken seriously – they were, as Matisse later put it, "a distraction". But with her generous gesture, Anna unknowingly ended her son's precious law career. "Once bitten by the demon of painting," Matisse later wrote, "I never wanted to give up." He went back to be a lawyer's clerk but was as bored as ever – in art, he had found something far more fulfilling and consuming than law. Without his father's knowledge, he enrolled in art classes before and after work, often rising before dawn and eating late dinners in pitch darkness. Ten years later, at the age of thirty, he had dropped law altogether and was studying art in Paris.

From then on, art took precedence over all his worldly ties. When he and his wife Amélie were first together, Matisse told her, "I love you dearly mademoiselle, but I shall always love painting more". Conceited as this sounds, it was honest: painting was a passion that gripped Matisse all his life. If he didn't paint, he was jumpy and prickly – only the violin could ease his nerves (he sometimes played non-stop, for hours on end). While he spoke of it in a modest middle-class way – "like a good armchair in which to rest from physical fatigue" – his thirst for art was anything but humble. He imposed harsh and exacting standards on himself and others, working almost every day of his life. He described the holy grail of his endeavours as "a higher ideal of beauty".

An unexpected freedom

Matisse's commitments are easily taken for Romantic idealism, but behind his priorities were the very specific rewards of the artistic enterprise – a psychological payoff that was more valuable than the stable income of a legal career. As he saw it, art allowed him to express his unique perceptions and emotions, transforming the tangle of private life into a crisp and clear public document. Matisse's works all embody his vivid vision of the world, what he called his "religious feeling ... towards life". Half a century since his death, this feeling remains in his painting, sculptures and decoupage. A good example is *The Rose Marble Table*, which he painted during the catastrophe of the First World War. While crammed into the frame, the table isn't claustrophobic – it's all open-air coolness and freshness. Crisp apples cluster near a rustic basket, and the table is luminescent against the dark, dappled dirt beneath. Amid the vines and nearby trees, there is an atmosphere of shaded intimacy and repose. The work is enlivening, suffused with a calm but genuine exuberance. "I am unable to distinguish," he wrote in 1908, "between the feeling I have for life, and my way of expressing it." In this way, the painting isn't just a representation of furniture and food. It's an offering, of sorts – of everyday wonder and gratitude.

But what is fascinating about Matisse's paintings is not just this captivating, compulsive vision of life; it's also that his career happened at all. All the strongest psychic and social forces were pushing him towards law and middle-class respectability. His parents were supporting him emotionally and financially to graduate and earn a living. His peers were studying and working their way towards graduation and employment. Bourgeois France was urging him to join their ranks, while brutal economic realities necessitated a steady income. Law was the safe choice: the path of a good son, husband and citizen. It wasn't until illness intervened that he was given respite from his duties and obligations. What he and his mother thought was a "distraction" was actually a liberation – the slow but serious emancipation of his character. It became the bluebird he chased until his death. "Before I had no interest in anything," he said. "From the moment I held that box of colours in my hand, I knew this was my life ... It was a tremendous attraction, a sort of Paradise Found in which I was completely free, alone, at peace."

The philosopher and social critic Herbert Marcuse would not have been shocked by Matisse's struggles or his aesthetic epiphanies.

Like many in the influential Frankfurt School, Marcuse argued that day-to-day life was one of fixed and narrow horizons. The necessities of life are indifferent to our aspirations for happiness. In *One Dimensional Man*, first published in the 1960s, Marcuse wrote of an age of "total mobilisation", where governments, corporations and the media fashion a seamless world of facts and truisms, and the weasel words that unthinkingly speak these. So-called "habits of thought" appear, which refuse questioning and stifle imagination. "Autonomy, discovery, demonstration, and critique," wrote Marcuse, "all recede before designation, assertion, and imitation." If Matisse lived in simpler times, he was no doubt bound by very similar kinds of repression and marginalization. It was taken for granted that he would serve the legal apparatus of France, without questioning the State or its laws. Even if his boredom was a nascent radicalism in the midst of this, he would still be, in Marcuse's words, "quickly digested by the status quo".

For Marcuse, art was a way out of the trap: a glimpse of a better life. But it wasn't a panacea or balm for him. It wasn't a mere distraction, in other words. "Art's unique truth," he wrote in *The Aesthetic Dimension*, "breaks with both everyday reality and holiday reality." He argued that art contains all the emotions and sensations of real life yet gives them a new form and medium. This is what Marcuse called "aesthetic form": the unique character of art, where the familiar and the forgotten are put before us with freshness and vividness. Art makes "the petrified world speak, sing, perhaps dance". Some decades before Marcuse, Matisse recognized this quite clearly. A lady once criticized his portraits, saying something like, "I never saw a woman like that." "Madam," he replied calmly, "that is not a woman; it is a painting." As lines, colours, curves or textures, art doesn't try to replace reality, nor does it try to repress it – it is its own reality, that of show, appearance and semblance. If it allows us to see things freshly, it does so without claiming to be anything other than a work of art. And like Matisse's disfigured women, all good art is beautiful in its own way – even the ugliest art can have a compelling vigour. In this guise, it allows us to experience a kind of "double sight": one eye on what is and was, and another on what might be or should be. Some of the finest works reveal death in a world of preserved or statistical corpses, love in a world of hatred or mutual use, and memory among forgetfulness.

Matisse's painting *The Dance* is an arresting example of this transformation. Painted to decorate the house of the Russian industrialist and collector Sergei Shchukin, it has what Matisse called a "Dionysian" mood: its wild, frenzied maenads are a world away from the tame bacchants of popular nineteenth-century art. A powerful rejection of the tricks and tropes of academic painting, Robert Hughes spoke of it as "one of the few wholly convincing images of physical ecstasy made in the twentieth century". In a climate of conservatism, this was a jolt of joy, abandon and carnality. But it was achieved with painterly restraint. The work expresses a wild pagan celebration with the elegance, harmony and beauty of classical art. The bodies of the dancers glow, their skin hot and red against the cool blue of the sky. Their faces are contorted, heads and bodies twisted, almost to the point of ugliness – but the flowing rhythm of their joined arms and curved figures, and the sharp delineation of colour and line, give the work an intense beauty. Instead of repressing passion and instinct, it harmonizes them with clarity, order and reason. In this way, Matisse gave Shchukin a picture of ecstatic freedom. His "aesthetic form" wasn't trying to copy or obscure the world – it was a world of its own, with its own rules and necessities. In this sense, it was pure freedom, exactly as Matisse intuited and Marcuse theorized.

It might seem dubious and even absurd to see Matisse through the eyes of the Marxist Marcuse. After all, Matisse was the painter of odalisques for bourgeois boudoirs. He was the neurotic and well-educated Hugh Hefner of French Post-Impressionism, who worked in his blue pyjamas, surrounded by naked models. But the seemingly conservative Matisse was reviled by many of his contemporaries – he wasn't the "King of the Beasts", the Fauves, for nothing. His works were laughed at and jeered at by the public and scorned by the establishment. Even the Post-Impressionists had their moments of cruelty – Paul Sérusier, a friend of Gauguin, told the painter Maurice Denis: "When a boy scrawls shit on a wall, he may be expressing himself ... but it's not a work of art". As it happens, the German artist Anton Henning *did* make an abstract work with his own faeces, and it *was* seen as art, but this was many decades too late to console Matisse. When the obstinate Frenchman chose to develop his own idiosyncratic style, he turned his back on self-congratulation and self-righteousness and on the paintings that celebrated them. In doing so, he refused to be bound by common or popular ways of seeing and feeling; he liberated perception and emotion without succumbing to idle fantasies or histrionics. He was crushing an old "tyranny of form", as Marcuse put it, and imposing his own.

Matisse's emancipation from an oppressive career to radicalism was occasioned by happenstance: an illness, and a brief encounter with pigment on canvas. And in many ways, his career change could only be a matter of luck, combined with stubborn opportunism. For his parents and peers, art was a superfluity – a luxury that didn't belong in the universe of the practically minded. But as Marcuse suggested, the significance of art isn't its pecuniary recompense or guarantee of esteem. Instead, and at its best, its value is its contribution to the breadth and depth of human experience. Rather than aping the status quo or offering a comforting opportunity for denial, it can be transformative. It works with the experiential fabric of reality to induce profound and diverse encounters with ourselves and the world. In doing so, it not only offers intensely enjoyable experiences but also encourages the discovery and celebration of freedom. And this is precisely what the young Matisse found in his box of paints. His experience suggests that art is not a diversion but a vivid and compelling path to self-possession. If we can't all be professional artists, we can certainly seek this distinctive liberty in a more attuned perception and in lively imagination. Given the attention it deserves, art is no mere diversion – it can liberate us from life's commonplace distractions.

Looking more closely

But sadly, many of our encounters with wonderful art are duds: some of the finest collections in the world can leave us cold. And it's not for want of goodwill or information. All the signs and plaques alert us to the masterpieces in our midst, but we find them as arresting and inspiring as a tepid cup of tea. Put simply, art promises a great deal but it doesn't always deliver. And often this is because we're distracted by our own inherited and educated preconceptions.

When my wife and I visited the National Gallery on our first trip to London, I experienced precisely this let-down. We were excited by the impressive array of historic and contemporary works, most of which we had previously seen only in reproductions. I was particularly looking forward to the work of van Gogh, whom I saw as the perfect poster boy for the Romantic artist: unrecognized and psychologically unstable, but a genuinely radical innovator. Having read all about the Expressionist movement, I was expecting to be awestruck and edified by its profundity. But when I encountered his famous *Sunflowers*, I was disappointed. To my naïve eye, it seemed small, drab and clumsily executed – the work of a novice, not a great master. The brilliant simplicity of his framing, and his wonderfully tactile use of colour, stroke and shade, were lost on me. Instead of a life-changing epiphany, I had found a sandy-coloured object, and an unremarkable one at that. My visit's supposed apex was actually a dismal failure – I was unable to enjoy the work of a genius, and I felt foolish.

Some of the most intelligent and urbane artists and scholars of recent history have had similar experiences. What's common is an inability to overcome education and training, to resist the baggage of entrenched knowledge. A telling example is given by the novelist and philosopher Marcel Proust. In his narrator's muddled attempts to enjoy and understand art, we're offered not only a fascinating insight into the obstacles to aesthetic appreciation but also a fine demonstration of how these are removed. The key to enjoying art isn't simply in formal education or the accumulation of historical facts. On the contrary, these are often a distraction from what art offers. As Marcel eventually grasped (with a little help from a famous painter), to enjoy the benefits of art, what is crucial is intelligent, imaginative attention.

The young Proust was smart, sensitive and sickly – perfect for a career as an author. Plagued by asthma, hay fever and other illnesses, he spent many days resting: reading, writing and in reverie. In his wonderful essay *On Reading*, he reminisced about his childhood devotion to books and on the places and times with which they intertwined. "There are perhaps no days of our childhood we lived so fully," he wrote, "as those we left without having lived them, those we spent with a favourite book." He spoke about vacations spent indoors with books; and of the quiet when the household went for a walk, when he'd curl up on a chair in the dining room, next to the smoky wood fire.

He would never have made a good sportsman or soldier; even a military desk job was out of the question – his handwriting was appalling, so the army bureaucracy wouldn't have him. But help was at hand to extend the young aesthete's shrinking horizons. His maternal grandmother, Adèle Weil, whom he adored, was robust and outdoorsy, as well as intelligent and literary. Proust loved nature from afar, whereas she threw herself into it with gusto. In one lovely passage of his opus, the narrator's grandmother happily went for a stroll in the rain, the servants thinking her "a bit off her head". In

Remembrance of Things Past, it was Adèle (or "Mme Amédée") who took her sickly young grandson to Balbec, where he had his first (and most famous) dud encounter with great art.

Balbec was a fictional holiday town on the Brittany coast, probably based on Cabourg, where the older Proust spent his summers. As a young man, "Marcel" (Proust gave the narrator his own name) was told about the violent storms and seas of the Brittany coast. To him, this seemed to be the epitome of nature's excellence: wild, romantic, violent, beautiful and terrible. When he asked a family friend about Balbec, he was told that this rugged seaside coast was also the home of the Balbec Cathedral, a towering Gothic church. Marcel imagined that its glorious spires were rooted in the coastline itself, the magnificent carvings and sculptures rising up from the scraggy rocks of the sea. He was taken to see reproductions of the cathedral's statues and longed to see and touch them. "I could scarcely breathe for joy," Proust wrote, "at the thought that I might myself, one day, see them take a solid form against their eternal background of salt fog." To Marcel, Balbec wasn't just a big church, an old relic on a hackneyed tourist route. It was a sublime vision of life itself, purified of all that was petty and poor. He lent to the name "Balbec" all sorts of fantasies: he imagined it as a quaint medieval town, still speaking archaic French, with an innkeeper who'd pour him coffee and milk, and take him to gaze at the sea. When his parents cautiously agreed to let Mme Amédée take him to Balbec, it was the promise of joy – a happiness worth the pain of travel. "Whatever it might be that I loved," he wrote, "it would never be attained save at the end of a long and heart-rending pursuit." While still weak and prone to asthma, the teenage Marcel bore horrible ills like a brief separation from his mother and a night in a strange bed (life was tough for the upper middle classes). For him, art was worth these agonies.

The trip to Balbec started well (Marcel got drunk on the train), but the young art lover was swiftly let down. Magically transported from his home town to Brittany, he found himself in a plain old railway station. There was no exotic mood to tell him it was Balbec, just a plain railway signpost. He asked the locals how to get to the beach, so he could "see nothing in the place but its church and the sea", but they were baffled. The cliffs and ocean spray were twelve miles away – there was neither shore nor harbour in Old Balbec. Instead of rising majestically from the rocks, the church stood near the railway station, next to tram lines. A billiard hall was nearby, and the statues were covered in the same soot as the houses. The Porch of the Virgin, which he had idolized, sat contaminated by the nearby election placard, bus office and bank; it smelled like a bakery. Marcel was bitterly dissatisfied and disillusioned. He tried to console himself with the authenticity of the place ("now it is the church itself, the statue itself; these are they; they, the unique things") but he couldn't fool himself. His sacrosanct vision of the cathedral was gone. Ordinary life had trespassed on the sacred grove of art.

For French sociologist Pierre Bourdieu, this is a typically bourgeois idea of art. In his seminal work of sociology *Distinction* (and unlike Marcuse and Matisse), Bourdieu set out to reveal the social reality behind the myths of art. While the art world treats art as if it were above and beyond everyday life, Bourdieu saw it as a battleground of class and status. In other words, art is a way to gain distinction: recognition, prestige, authority and so on; when we acquire a work of art, we are making an investment – we're hoping our good taste will be revealed and our cultural stock will rise. And this war (for what Bourdieu calls "capital") is won by fleeing from anything that smacks of hard work and everyday pathos. For example, those with the most capital in the art world enjoy the most abstract, minimal art. For Bourdieu, there's a very simple logic at work here: the more someone accumulates money or leisure, the less they need to slave and drudge. Their interest in art derives from an interest in a life of purity and freedom, with no need for anything practical or useful. In this way, their seemingly pure taste is actually a kind of social game, a play for the top of the social ladder. For those on the bottom rung (without money or *savoir faire*), the art world is closed altogether. Theirs is a life of necessity, in which art and style are luxuries. In between the avant-garde and the proles are the middling classes with their safe Impressionism and a whole constellation of other tastes. For all of these art lovers, the same myth remains: art is beyond the economic, social or political necessities of life and can't be sullied by everyday cares. Whether it is worshipped in the giant cathedrals of the middle classes ("The Impressionists: 1st June – 31st December – Buy Tickets Now!") or the private chapels of the *haute bourgeoisie* (a Watteau in the dining room), art is a religion: a faith, complete with priests, prayers and pilgrims.

If Bourdieu is right, young Marcel's trip to Balbec was a failed gambit, a player's tactic that backfired. His hopes for an otherworldly artistic epiphany were thoroughly in line with his class, status and snobbery. As a young upper-middle-class gentleman, he longed for art devoid of everyday grind and urban grime; he dreamed up other-worldly spectres, without the minutiae and mess of real life. This was all perfectly prestigious, as was his sincerity and gravity ("one of the preconditions of successful investment," wrote Bourdieu). It's just that he farcically forgot to play the game properly. He got too carried away and allowed his fantasies to get the better of him – we might say that he wasn't quite cynical enough. Of course, the older Proust (the obsessive recluse who wrote *Remembrance of Things Past*) was not so innocent. He knew all about the bourgeois games of social distinction, revealing them in his great novel with the skill of a forensic surgeon. This was why Bourdieu quoted him so often in *Distinction* – Proust "never ceased to cultivate and also analyse cultivated pleasure". But as a young man (or as "Marcel" in his novel), Proust was fervently and guilelessly clinging to the art world's fantasy, what Bourdieu called "the denial of the social". Fed by books and photos that robbed art of anything that might pollute aesthetic purity – like ordinary scenery, bodily lust, economic exploitation – Marcel's imagination soared. The fictional Marcel's investment in the game (what Bourdieu calls the *illusio*, "the fact of being caught up in and by the game") was badly spent. His daydreams were tarnished, and he was left feeling foolish.

Nowadays, Bourdieu's ideas can be quite consoling: they suggest that our disappointing experiences of art are commonplace and out of our hands. In renowned art galleries all over the world, visitors are sold on artistic glamour and genius. There are promises of "breathtaking", "astonishing" and "once-in-a-lifetime" experiences ("fear of loss", they call this in door-to-door advertising). They sell the bourgeois dream of pure, transcendent art. But once we've braved the long queues and forked out cash for family tickets, the sheen quickly wears off. The gallery is noisy and crowded, and the paintings are hidden by bored security guards and velvet ropes. And even when we're not distracted by chatty guides or restless schoolkids ticking boxes on assignments, there are too many paintings anyway. Our eyes listlessly flit over each painting for about seventeen seconds, we read the program or label, then move on. By the time we've seen twenty masterpieces and read thirty curatorial explanations, we're physically and mentally exhausted (victims of what the psychologist Edward Robinson called "museum fatigue"). And we've *still* not had the climactic encounter promised by the advertisements.

Bourdieu's fieldwork suggests that these flat experiences aren't just born of ignorance, stupidity or faithlessness (as if we're not pious enough for the gods of art); instead, they're part of a much broader and deeper conflict of status and class. People from well-to-do or educated families might like to enjoy Watteau or Rothko but are put off by the noise and mess of the everyday. They find many of today's art museums patronizing and vulgar. Lower-class folk often find themselves alienated by the same places and avoid them altogether; they see them as "snobby", "up themselves", "arty-farty". Meanwhile, there are the avant-garde who find museums staid and dull, and the middling classes who worship all things artistic but are baffled by everything before da Vinci and after Monet. In other words, there's nothing mysterious about bad art experiences (ours or Marcel's) – they're just a matter of breeding and education and can be easily mapped-out on a sociological matrix. No matter who we are, we are somewhere in Bourdieu's descriptions and diagrams. If we pay good money for art blockbusters and come away flat, it's probably just because we're too high-class (or not high-class enough).

This certainly seems to be the case with Marcel Proust. His education was, of course, excellent: Greek, Latin, French, the classics, science and philosophy. For years he wasn't the best student in class (the grandiloquent dandy missed many days to sickness), but he was known to be an intelligent, curious and brilliant writer. By the time he graduated from his *lycée*, he was good enough to win the coveted *Prix d'honneur de dissertation française*. As a young man, he enrolled at the university in law and international politics, and he graduated in 1893. Soon after, he badgered his parents to let him study philosophy. "Even in my most desperate moments," he wrote to his father, "I can't conceive of anything more odious than becoming a lawyer." But if the fictional Marcel was indeed a version of his younger self, Proust's fine education wasn't enough to save him from his Balbec farce. If anything, his idealistic education worsened it, and this is classic Proust: a snob who exposes snobbery, an idealist who exposes idealism. As with Proust at the *lycée*, upbringing and schooling might introduce students to the "right" tastes in art, food, clothes and ideas but it can't always help them enjoy these. They become aesthetes, but without the fine aesthetic experiences this entails. To learn new ways of appreciating paintings, sculptures, compositions and works of architecture (as the older Proust did), a different kind of education is needed.

In *Remembrance of Things Past*, it wasn't a university professor or *lycée* teacher who educated Marcel about Balbec's beauty. It was the painter Elstir. In the chapter "Seascape, With a Frieze of Girls", Marcel and his friend Saint-Loup saw Elstir in a little seaside restaurant and eagerly wrote him a letter outlining their passionate admiration for his work (neither had seen his paintings). The old painter graciously invited Marcel to his studio. He found the painter's neighbourhood and house vulgar ("I made an effort … not to see the gimcrack splendour of the buildings"), but he was impressed by the old man's insights. Proust described him as a man with a "highly cultivated mind", who was nevertheless able to put aside his intellectual prejudices and look carefully at nature and art.

When Marcel mentioned his disappointments at the Porch of the Virgin at Balbec, Elstir was aghast. He lovingly described the building's sculptures to Marcel, rapturously praising their profundity and beauty. He lauded the humility of the angels carrying the Virgin, and the modesty of the Madonna. In one particularly touching passage, Elstir spoke about the depiction of Resurrection Day. Instead of an abstract theological rendering, the Balbec artist portrayed a husband helping his wife out of her grave. As she is worried and scared, he holds her hand against his heart to show that it's beating. "Is that such a trumpery idea," he asked his young guest, "do you think, so stale and commonplace?" While clearly well versed in theology and biblical exegesis, the painter was undistracted by his high-minded ideas and unperturbed by the grime and tackiness of old Balbec town.

The crucial thing about Elstir wasn't *savoir faire* or some typically Romantic indignation towards harsh reality. He wasn't suggesting that art was somehow outside the everyday world (with all its shortcomings). His lesson to Marcel wasn't one of snobbery, quietism, apolitical conservatism or other-worldly asceticism. Rather than thinking his way into the bas-reliefs and statues with philosophy, theology or sociology, Elstir treated them as an invitation. Balbec offered an exciting and enticing combination of sensations: textures, colours, forms, lines, and the symbols and narratives they suggested. Taking up the invitation, the old painter gave these qualities his careful attention and allowed the sensations and perceptions to fire his imagination. It was then that his keen intellect could do its work (but not before). To educate Marcel, he didn't lecture him on Thomas Aquinas and St Augustine. He simply demonstrated that the best way to enjoy an artwork was sensitive, imaginative attention – something we're all capable of, if we have the time, energy and inclination.

Yet there is a philosophy at work here – and one helpful for overcoming the distractions of art, and the art world. In Marcel's failure and Elstir's wonder, Proust gave a memorable depiction of two opposing urges in the human mind. There's our imagination, which is active: it loves to expand, impose its own mental order and create fictions with which to play. There's also sensation, which is passive: it accepts the necessity of the outside world and has little of its own creation. Our intellect accommodates both these urges. It can aid imagination in its flights of fancy, or it can bow to the reality our senses perceive, fixing and narrowing a world of facts. In Balbec, Marcel was torn between imagination and sensation, intellectual creativity and intellectual precision. He wanted to allow his mind to wander, but part of him also wanted to cling to his preconceptions. He was struggling to find the right attention, the right concentration, without being distracted by his own fancies, or intellectual prejudices or the sensory flood of the town.

The philosopher and poet Friedrich Schiller wrote of a very similar struggle. In *On the Aesthetic Education of Man*, he argued that mankind is always mediating between two basic impulses. There is a sensuous impulse, which is material, tangible, wedded to the muck and tumble of everyday life. Then there is a formal impulse, which is intangible, ideal and perfect. The first is heightened by culture to become a sensitive and open feeling. The second is educated to become intellectual clarity and coherence. When these two impulses are violently opposed, they run rampant. Intellect runs away with itself, creating baseless phantoms or robbing reality of its sensuous richness. Or the sensuous impulse creates beasts of us – creatures of pure feeling, without reason. Left to ourselves, we are divided, slightly schizoid creatures.

For Schiller, the aim was to bring these into harmony, and this could be achieved through art. Art combines the sensuous and the ideal. To enjoy art, we must allow ourselves to be led by the richness of our senses, but then we must also unite these feelings with the products of our minds. We find order, pattern, line, colour, shape, and we employ our imaginations. Our sensuous impulse seeks life: all that is organic, physical, tangible. Our formal impulse seeks shape: all that is ordered, coherent, delineated. The finest art combines both of these in "living shape" – in other words, beauty. For Schiller, beauty was not pretty things or sexy bodies – it was the combination of material colour, texture and other "stuff" with the forms that hold them. Our aim is to find both of these in art and to allow our mind to revel in both. Our mind rests as sensation flows over it, and is active as it plays with what it sees. When we are enjoying art in this way, we're not trying to restrain our senses, nor are we reining in our mind. Instead, by allowing our senses to fully enjoy what is before us and allowing our imagination to work upon the artwork, we're reconciling our faculties in a single object. As he wrote, "through beauty the sensuous man is led to form and to thought; through beauty the spiritual man is brought back to matter and restored to the world of sense." This, for Schiller, was "play" – the perfect unity of impulses, which encapsulates the fullest of human sensitivity and creativity. By drawing on our finest impulses working in a playful union, art cultivates our humanity.

When we are playing we needn't fear (as Marcel did) the clash between art and reality, sensation and imagination, intellect and emotion, dreams and waking life. In play, each impulse strives to its fullest, without overstepping its bounds. And this is precisely why Elstir wasn't afraid to imagine, to speculate and to invent. "When the mind has a tendency to dream," he said to Marcel, "it is a mistake to keep dreams away from it, to ration its dreams. So long as you distract your mind from its dreams, it will not know them for what they are; you will always be being taken in by the appearance of things, because you will not have grasped their true nature." Art lets truth be truth and dreams be dreams – there's no conflict or vagueness between reality and semblance (Schiller was an obvious influence on Marcuse).

Even if Schiller's claims sound like Romantic hyperbole (Bourdieu would not approve), *On the Aesthetic Education of Man* is a brilliant guide to the appreciation and enjoyment of art. It suggests that we don't try to fix, once and for all, the precise nature of every work. We don't need to predetermine it with intellect: we can put aside our knowledge of history, philosophy, economics and politics, if only for a little while. But neither do we want to simply give in to a flood of sensations: the guides, the iPods, the echoes and chatter of the gallery, or the grime and banality of the city. Like Proust, Schiller was suggesting that we simply pay sensitive and mindful attention. We allow our senses to take in the details, then we let our minds go to work. The intellect will think about issues and themes, our emotions will be fired and our imaginations will be lost in rich reverie. But these are kept in check by lively sensation, which is bringing our faculties back to what we see. There is a delicious to and fro between the work of our minds and the flow of our eyes. The finest works of art are those that fire both impulses – they are a feast for our sight and a cooling drink for our rampant intellect. They offer us rich and nuanced objects for our imagination to play with, leading to intense interest, captivation and satisfaction. They allow us, as adults, to learn as children learn: in serious play. To avoid distraction's embarrassments and disappointments, we don't need any esoteric secrets, codes or stunning facts – we just have to look a little more closely.

The courageous gaze

At its best, art can challenge the limits of our daily lives; it offers encounters of rare nuance and intensity. In simple terms, art enriches and clarifies our life – it's an antidote to distraction and the disorientation that often comes with it. But this lucidity isn't always easy to face. Even if we're able to avoid the diversions of formal education and ambient noise, we don't always *want* to see what art affords us. If we're afraid of change, or anxious about our own proclivities, it's easy to narrow our perception and restrict our imagination. And this is worse when life is difficult. When the work of art offers a glimpse of something pleasing, we sometimes grip these impressions a little too tightly, refusing more unsettling interpretations. We filter out anything that is confronting or disturbing. The danger is that this becomes a barren fanaticism – we unknowingly impoverish our own experience and the possibilities for thought and feeling that this experience affords. And this often has nothing to do with intelligence or sincerity.

A telling example is the German philosopher Martin Heidegger. Heidegger's writings on art have been immensely influential in contemporary aesthetics and environmentalism, overshadowing much of his earlier (and perhaps more straightforward) philosophy. And they certainly merit this authority. But they also reveal the danger of narrowing our aesthetic gaze, particularly on those occasions when art has afforded us asylum, a sanctuary from the complications of life. In such cases, art offers intense and wonderful experience, but we're unable to shake the impressions closest to us. As a result, our encounters become restricted and dogmatic – in a word, anaesthetized to novelty and diversity.

To appreciate Heidegger's contributions and shortcomings, it's best to place him in his philosophical context. A legendary anecdote will suffice. Some time between 1921 and 1922, a group of students sat down in a classroom of Germany's Freiburg University. The topic for the course was Aristotle, and the lecturer was a young Martin Heidegger. Like many teachers, he began with a brief biographical sketch. But instead of whetting his pupils' appetites with a rollicking *Bildungsroman* story, he simply said of the great Aristotle: "He was born, worked and died". For this young lecturer, what was important was Aristotle's thought, not the petty details of his life. Indeed, his life *was* his work.

As the anecdote suggests, Heidegger wasn't a part-time thinker or pop writer – he was a philosopher's philosopher. He avoided the day-to-day cares of the common man and his so-called "common sense". "Overcoming common sense," wrote Heidegger in *An Introduction to Metaphysics*, "is the first step of philosophy." For him, philosophy wasn't about food prices, birthdays or the minutiae of family life. It was about thought, pure and simple. Of course, we might say this of academia generally – it aspires to rise above our one-sided and narrow everyday life, to find more universal or precise truths. But Heidegger also had no truck with sociology, psychology or political science (which had lost their foundations), and certainly not with science. For Heidegger, these disciplines weren't as primordial as genuine philosophy. "The word *philosophia* appears," he wrote, "on the birth certificate of our own history." If academics are in an ivory tower above the masses Heidegger saw philosophy in the penthouse.

In his eyes, even more essential than philosophy was the philosopher himself. The ancient Greek word for this, as coined by Heraclitus, was *philosophos*. The *philosophos* wasn't just a scholar or intellectual in a modern university discipline – he was simply a lover of wisdom. In one work, Heidegger argued that the lover of wisdom was a man who desired the One beneath the Many, who longed to find the unity behind the diversity of the cosmos. He asked the fundamental "question of being". If everything in the universe is "being", what is this Being? What is it for something to "be"? This sounds like an abstract question, and it is. But it's a question all of us have answered in one way or another (even if we haven't asked it). We all have an idea of what it is for something to exist; for something to be, rather than not be at all. In *Being and Time*, Heidegger argued that our everyday lives are grounded in what he called our "stance on Being". We see the world in light of what we think it is to exist – we live in the light of Being. Indeed, for Heidegger the great epochs of history were partly determined by the "Being" of each – what they thought was *really* real. The Greeks saw Being as *physis*, the "rising in itself of all things". The Romans saw Being as *natura*, whence all things were born. Christians see Being as God. Many modern folk see Being as atoms, cells, precise forces: as the mathematical certainty of physics and other sciences. Of course, few have realized they have these ideas – most of us just going about our daily business, dealing with things in a matter-of-fact way. But for Heidegger, the task of the philosopher was to dig a little deeper. He believed that only the *philosophos* was "attuned to the voice of the Being of being".

Yet for the pious German professor, most philosophers had forgotten this question. In other words, most philosophers aren't philosophers – a characteristically Heideggerian conceit. Indeed, he suggested that the whole of Western civilization has forgotten it. We're no longer open to the question of Being – yes, we answer it in everything we do, but blithely and dimly. As Heidegger saw it, this amnesia was behind the ethical and political malaise of twentieth-century Europe. We treat the world as "stuff" to be manipulated and controlled, never stopping to ask questions of its basic nature. For something to "be", it just has to suit our frenzied plans: to be calculable, measurable, reliable. This logic of instrumentalism (Heidegger called it *Gestell*, "enframing") is at the heart of our ideas of Being and touches everything we say, think and do. The environment is "stuff" to be wood-chipped, flooded and mined, animals are "stuff" to be hunted and vivisected, and other humans are "stuff" to be exploited. And this idea of the world (what Heidegger called "technology") isn't something that follows political lines. For Heidegger, labels like "capitalism" and "communism" hid the fact that the entire modern world was in the grip of *Gestell*. "From a metaphysical point of view," he wrote in *An Introduction to Metaphysics*, "Russia and America are the same; the same dreary technological frenzy, the same unrestricted organisation of the average man." Both economies treat the world as a stockpile of "things" to be used and discarded, arranged and ordered (in the managerial, economic and military senses of the word). Blind to our own ideas of Being, we are destroying ourselves and taking the planet with us.

In the 1930s Heidegger, alienated by modernity, swallowed the panacea of many Germans: Nazism. His mentor and professorial colleague Edmund Husserl was Jewish, as were his lovers Elisabeth Blochmann and Hannah Arendt (the "saucy wood nymph" and "boisterous imp" of his letters). But this didn't stop Heidegger joining the Nazi party, happily lauding the Führer, and using "Jew" as a slur against an old colleague. As Rector of Freiburg University, he helped a few of his Jewish friends but alienated or isolated most and accepted Nazism's anti-Semitism without serious protest. In his 1933 rectorial address, he proclaimed the time was ripe for Germans to will their destiny, safely cocooned within their "spiritual–historical being" in Greece (only the Germans were the heirs to Greek thought). If the question of Being had been forgotten since Plato, the German university was going to recover and revivify itself and the nation, through united labour, military and intellectual services (a kind of philosophical boot camp). "German Students!" Rector Heidegger later wrote in a student newspaper, "Do not let principles and 'ideas' be the rules of your being. The Führer himself ... is the German reality of today, and of the future, and of its law ...

Heil Hitler!" Colleagues like the celebrated Karl Jaspers were aghast at this wholehearted embrace of Nazism. Jaspers asked Heidegger how a boor like Hitler could rule Germany. "Culture is of no importance," Heidegger replied, "look at his marvellous hands!" For Heidegger, Hitler's charisma and charm were more important than brainpower. After all, with their brutal intellectualism, scholars had forgotten Being for millennia. Hitler was the promise of a new age of soil, folk and divinity, purified of all that was mechanistic, scientific and technological.

This promise was broken – tragically so. Either through pathological gullibility or denial, Heidegger had betrayed many of his own principles (to say nothing of his colleagues and fellow Germans). Nazism was just as relentless and exacting as modern science and bureaucracy, wedded to incalculable brutality. The planet was just a "standing reserve", ready and available to be gathered up, processed and exploited. Heidegger himself hinted at this with his remark that agriculture was "a motorized food industry, the same thing in its essence as the production of corpses in the gas chambers and the extermination camps". Everything became "stuff" for Germany to control and manipulate: minerals and metals for tanks and bullets, food and water for its armies, and the Germans themselves, who worked in homes, factories and armies for the glory of the Reich. The peoples of Austria and the *Sudetenland* were annexed to the Third Reich, while the Jews of Europe were treated like "human resources": brutally collected, distributed and discarded. This wasn't a new era of proud *Volk* – it was aggressive modern imperialism, fired by racism, nationalism, and pre-war poverty and humiliation. Heidegger's grandiose ideas of the "destiny of Being" were fictions, alien to the machine of Nazi Germany. At best, they were naïve fantasies; at worst, cynical propaganda. And these ideas provided the conditions for Heidegger's flight to art.

To the grave disappointment of some and the disgust of others, the famous professor never apologized, or even lamented his political corruption (which some saw as petty opportunism, others as deeply ingrained anti-Semitism, nationalism and conservatism). For years he kept silent, only occasionally touching upon his wartime Nazism. Just after the war, he wrote a little essay entitled "The Rectorate 1933/34: Facts and Thoughts", in which he sketched out his politics and their philosophical justifications. For the most part, it painted him as an academic Quixote, trying to lend sincerity and authenticity to the National Socialist movement and help his Jewish friends. There was no apology, no lamentation of Hitler's atrocities and certainly nothing like a mature self-examination. And many of Heidegger's other statements after the war were equally inadequate. His interview with the German weekly *Der Spiegel*, which was published posthumously in 1976, had its down-to-earth moments (he admitted "human failure" stopped him visiting his mentor Husserl on his death bed) but was profoundly disappointing overall. He gave the same impression of a guileless do-gooder, trying to save Nazism from the Nazis – the interview barely touches on his own guilt or culpability. George Steiner, whose book *Heidegger* is a generous testament to the philosopher's brilliance, still speaks of Heidegger's "feline urbanity and evasions", and "intolerable" post-war silence. For many Europeans, Professor Heidegger was a traitor, an anti-Semite and an academic charlatan, hiding his wartime evils with pettifoggery. In a heartfelt and angry letter from America, Heidegger's own student Herbert Marcuse accused him of being "outside Logos" – beyond the world of rationality and reason.

But Heidegger never turned back to Marcuse's "Logos". He barely commended or recommended the philosophical vocation, at least as his peers would have understood it. "Philosophy will not be able to bring about a direct change of the present state of the world," he told *Der Spiegel*. Rejecting any sort of human endeavour, he turned to what seemed like quietism and aesthetics: "Only a god can still save us. I think the only possibility of salvation left to us is to prepare readiness, through thinking and poetry, for the god or for the absence of the god during the decline." Alongside his "thinking" (which many saw as mysticism), Heidegger nominated poetry. And indeed, a central theme in Heidegger's middle and late works was art. While he spoke of poetry, by this he meant *poiesis*, the old Greek word for making, shaping, building (today, the Greek word for baker is still *artopoios*, "bread maker"). For him, true poetry was a kind of shaping, building, crafting that created whole new ways of life. Homer and Hesiod shaped the world of the ancient Greeks, and we might say that Shakespeare did the same for England. And by "poetry", Heidegger didn't just mean words on a page. While he thought poetry to be the purest art, he spoke of all artists as poets. Sculpture and painting were as much poetry as the lines of the Germanic writers Rilke or Hölderlin.

But Heidegger's most arresting, illuminating discussion of art was of something different altogether: ancient Greek architecture. In his "Origin of the Work of Art" (written when he was disillusioned by Nazism), he wrote of a temple at Paestum, a Greek colony in southern Italy. While the Parthenon in Athens lies in ruins, the temple at Paestum sits proudly on its stone throne, shining against the Mediterranean sky. Lichen grows on its columns, like coral on a sunken ship, and a few ruins seem to sprout from the surrounding grass, just as wildflowers bloom nearby. For Heidegger, this was true art – art that speaks of Being. He wrote: "The lustre and gleam of the stone ... first brings to light the light of the day, the breath of the sky, the darkness of the night." Heidegger also spoke of the temple revealing the firmness of the rock, the rush of the storm, and the surge of the surf. For him, the temple wasn't simply a work; not a thing, a bit, a chunk. It was a work of art because it was working for the Greeks who dwelt in Paestum; "work" was a verb, not a noun. It worked by allowing the strife between things to come forth: the strife between lightness and dark, movement and stillness, visibility and invisibility, openness and closedness, and so on. Yet it could only allow this strife to be revealed because these things weren't really cleaved apart – the lightness of the marble needed the darkness of the sky, just as the movement of the sea needed the stillness of the stone. As Heidegger put it, the "rock comes to bear and rest, and so first becomes rock; metals come to glimmer and shimmer, colours to glow". In short, all these things need one another to be what they are. The temple is a work of art because it reveals this need: the play of all things.

In the play of Paestum, Heidegger gave an arresting answer to the question: What can help Western civilization out of its malaise? The temple was a work of art because it worked to reveal the differences in things that made these things what they were. Moreover, this wasn't simply how things looked; it wasn't an illusion or magic trick. Instead, Heidegger was saying that this strife between things was the basic way of the world. As we saw earlier, he wrote approvingly of the Greek idea of Being, *physis*: "the rising in itself of all things". For Heidegger, Being is exactly this falling and rising, lightening and darkening, hiding and revealing – all things that *are* are this movement. So as a work of art, the Paestum temple is not only revealing the world of the Greeks, it is also bringing to light the world itself. Indeed, this "bringing to light" is also *physis*: a revealing of things. In one of those twists philosophers delight in, the temple is revealing the true nature of the world as *physis* by being *physis*. For Heidegger, this was the work of art, hard at work revealing Being. And revealing Being (in this way, at least) was a shining path to the redemption of the West.

Intriguing though this is to my jaded modern ears, Heidegger's aesthetic philosophy remains tainted with fascism. Most obviously, his prose has the hypnotic tone of a dictatorial monologue: "Out of the mirroring mirror-play the thinging of the thing takes place." Dr Heidegger has had the same effect on adults as Dr Seuss has on children: a kind of academic mesmerism, where the rhythm and metre of the words lead to a trance of philosophical reverie. And there's a dark side to this poetic rambling. In his penchant for reading authoritative statements from long-dead Greeks ("exegesis" in the academic parlance), Heidegger was avoiding debate and discussion. While several of his letters and seminars have been published, there's still a totalitarian mood to his work; a mode of address that suggests charisma and authority, instead of appeal to reason, rationality and logic (one student spoke of his lectures as like a "political rally", where "contemptuous epigrams" sting the ears of all but the "blessed few"). It's difficult to envisage Heidegger hurling himself into the fray of political dialogue or debate, or patiently dealing with the objections of critics. Indeed, after his disastrous (and sometimes farcical) flirtations with Nazism, Heidegger's aesthetics seem like a flight from all the mess and fuss of the real world – a diversion or distraction from what haunted him.

There's also a painful echo of other-worldliness in his aesthetics. He gave art a grand mission by wedding it to Being, his lifelong study. But in doing so, he scorned most of the world's great masterworks: if they didn't reveal "the Being of beings", then they weren't truly art. In this way, art became yet another in a long line of Heideggerian abstractions – purities untouched and unsullied by real life. Perhaps the best example was his vision of Paestum itself. Travelling at Paestum for the first time, the great German writer Johann Wolfgang von Goethe told his readers to take their time among the Greek ruins. "It is only by walking through them and round them," he wrote in his *Italian Journey*, "that one can attune one's life to theirs and experience the emotional effect which the architect intended. I spent the whole day doing this." But Heidegger never took Goethe's advice. He visited Greece but not Paestum, and his sketch of the temple was, as far as we can tell, wholly imaginary. If Heidegger was part of a larger German tradition of inventing Greece from afar, he was a somewhat hypocritical member. As his student Marcuse bitterly observed years later, for all Heidegger's supposed earthiness and love of the land, in the end he was still spinning abstractions. As with Aristotle's biography, the facts and details of Paestum were irrelevant – insignificant and unnecessary detours on the road to Being.

Here there is a lesson for all art lovers. Heidegger's main problem wasn't that he was wrong about Being but that he saw it and nothing else. In other words, he took the truth he had discovered and he held on so tightly that he couldn't find any others. And Heidegger wasn't alone in this. For thousands of years, philosophers have found in art one thing, and then clung to this thing as the sole and sovereign truth of art. Plato saw art as dangerous copying, Aristotle as purging, Hegel as the manifestation of Spirit, and R. G. Collingwood as the expression of emotion. The problem with these thinkers wasn't that they were way off the mark – on the contrary, each hit upon something genuine in art or artists. The problem was that they took their bona fide insight and corrupted it by deifying it as a universal and eternal Truth of Art.

Because art is an industry, a great many professions also have a stake in partial visions of art. We've already seen philosophers succumb to narrowness, but the same is true for educators, businessmen and public servants. Mathematics teachers find spatial unities and trigonometric ratios in art, while history pedagogues find nascent battles or period dress. Corporations see inoffensive decoration and tax write-offs, while community advocates find a way to improve self-worth and social cohesion. And much of this works – art can be good for grades, the market and self-esteem. But the difficulty is that these professional biases can all too easily dominate experiences and the institutional conditions that shape them. Art is bought, sold, arranged and appreciated for its resale value, historical rarity or communal spirit, instead of its unique sensual contribution to life. Think of a milliner going to an expensive restaurant and ordering a sumptuous meal, then using it to make a hat – it might work fine, but it's a bloody waste of fine food.

We needn't be surprised by these oversights. There's a very good reason why they occur with art, particularly masterpieces. Because it fires our imaginations, it draws on all our personal passions, obsessions and blind spots. A brilliant work of art is easily Moby Dick to Ahab, God to Abraham and mass adoration to Paris Hilton. Heidegger could rightly see the play of Being in a Greek temple, where another Romantic might see picturesque ruins or the echoes of ancient gods. The great danger is that the imagined discoveries are so entrancing that they stifle creativity and open-mindedness. This is all the more likely when art is treated like a sanctuary, as it was for Heidegger. If work is stressful and unfulfilling, or domestic life is exhausting and unrecognized, art is an invitation to repose. If life seems unjust or unfair, art is a vision of righteousness or just deserts. If the city is ugly and barren, art can be beautiful and fecund. If the world seems nihilistic, art can be the abode of Being. And, no doubt, art is rich enough to bankroll all these fantasies, and more. But when our inclinations are all too easily met and satisfied, and our intellect stabilizes these gratifications, our urge to explore wanes. Our horizons narrow and we end up seeking what confirms our prejudices or quickly alters our mood (what R. G. Collingwood called "craft", not art). But by clinging to a one-sided appreciation of art, we impoverish our experience of life.

As Proust suggested in *Remembrance of Things Past*, to broaden and deepen our encounters with art requires neither high theory nor muddling through in a daze. What it requires is patient and sensitive attention to the sensory qualities a work has to offer – and this can occur at unexpected moments. As I write this, I'm sitting in a restaurant, overlooking a sculpture garden and an artificial pond. Above the green water, swaying European trees, and a large Balzac by Rodin, there is a huge expanse of sky. And in the middle of the blue are two whopping great industrial cranes – the sort used to construct high-rise buildings. Like many people, I find these things ugly, but strangely enough they actually add to this scene. Their stark, dark verticality highlights the bright openness of the sky and contrasts well against the soft foliage of the garden. If I had stuck to my prejudices, I would have overlooked this unexpected beauty and would not have enjoyed the idea it inspired (the charming unity of industrial and organic). Sometimes habits of perception can be pleasantly broken by a little attention in the right place.

Despite his enormous contribution to the philosophy of art, Heidegger refused this sort of openness. Confronted by the richness and diversity of aesthetic experience, he doggedly confined himself to the pursuit of Being. There's no doubt that his investigation of art was profound. But, in his weary flight from responsibility, Heidegger transformed art into a distraction: a receptacle for his safe abstractions, which diverted him from unwelcome ideas and emotions. In doing so, he robbed himself of the opportunity to refresh and revive his experience. This mistake can take many forms, but what is common is a refusal to see beyond the safety of a single insight: an unwillingness to face enigmatic and unknown possibilities. Even for the brightest, most sophisticated art lovers, sometimes what is needed is a more courageous gaze.

The Samurai's fan

Old age was taxing for Nikos Kazantzakis, the Greek poet, novelist and statesman – but he never lost his aesthetic bravery. A few years before he died, he was diagnosed with lymphatic leukaemia. Before Asiatic flu took his life, he suffered gangrene from a septic vaccination shot in China, the loss of his right eye to lymphatic disease, and the many other ailments of a well-travelled and hard-working septuagenarian. He was old and ill. Yet he kept writing. He spent hour upon hour with a pencil or pen in his hand, feverishly creating page after page of brilliant literature, poetry and philosophy. In a letter to a friend, he wrote: "I work many hours, and I don't get tired. This power of endurance alarms me; it isn't natural … The days seem short to me. The years I pass have never been shorter. I don't have enough time." When his right arm was gangrenous, he wrote left-handed. Clearly, pain and suffering were not enough to stop him doing his work. Indeed, three days before he died, Kazantzakis sent a congratulatory telegram to Albert Camus, who had just won the Nobel Prize for Literature. What made this particularly noble was that he himself was being considered for the prize – he lost at the last minute to the famous Frenchman. Kazantzakis loved art, in all its guises.

One of his most compelling reflections on art was inspired by his trip to Japan. Often baffled by the native customs and other curiosities, Kazantzakis was nonetheless compelled by their unique aesthetic sensibility. He spoke of the "deep spell, love and understanding, beauty and simplicity" of the humblest everyday things: boxes, knives, dolls, sandals. He told a particularly enchanting story about a trip to the Japanese theatre. While the tales were cliché, the performances moved him immensely, displaying an undeniable charm, elegance and potency. He wrote that the simplest detail was ripe with a rich balance of freedom and restraint, intoxication and sobriety. In particular, he recalled the fan held by a samurai on stage, which "becomes a living thing, an entity with a thousand faces, charming, challenging, threatening". For Kazantzakis, this was true art: the most modest of tools transformed into an expression of all the bittersweet richness of the human condition. The fan could simply be waved to and fro for coolness or coquetry, or it could be "a bird that opens and closes its wings and is lost, lightning that flashes its light on and off – red, green and blue, like a spirit". This is art not as a transcendent truth, or an amalgam of bits, but as a skill, a mood, and a subtlety of attention. This illuminates not only the chameleonic nature of things, but also the fragility of their artistry. If even the simplest thing can transform into a tool of art, then we can't be lax in our concentration and sensitivity. Art can come and go without pomp and ceremony, leaving us unaware of what we've lost. But the formula for enjoying this alchemy is remarkably simple – it's precisely what Kazantzakis evoked in the Japanese theatre: an artist who wields his tools with honesty and care, an audience with the sincere sensitivity to watch, listen and learn – and perhaps a writer to immortalize this magic. From these bonds come some of the most vivid, gripping and profound of life's metamorphoses.

6. The private life

The peace and prettiness of the whole land ... has been good to me, and I stay on with unabated relish. But I stay in solitude. I don't see a creature. That, too, dreadful to relate, I like.
  (Henry James, letter to Edmund Gosse, 28 August 1896)

We must know ... in our beautiful art, yours and mine, what we are talking about – and the only way to know is to have lived and loved and cursed and floundered and enjoyed and suffered.
  (Henry James, letter to Hugh Walpole, 21 August 1913)

For most of his life, the novelist Henry James was of no fixed address. He wasn't sleeping rough – far from it. The cosmopolitan Yankee lived in comfortable rooms, houses and hotels, often with servants. And perhaps he dreamt occasionally of a home of his own. "I have felt the all but irresistible desire," he wrote in a letter to a friend in Italy, "to put my hand on some modest pied-à-terre." But, as this suggests, he was looking for temporary accommodation, a small flat for Italian sun and fresh air. This rootlessness was something of a family trait. His father Henry Sr was a restive intellectual who dragged his young family all over Europe and the United States (James described himself and siblings as "hotel children"). When he matured, Henry Jr wrote, toured and dined in France, Italy, Switzerland and Ireland. He was, as Virginia Woolf put it, "of the tribes of wanderers and aliens; a winged visitant, ceaselessly circling and seeking, unattached, uncommitted." As a middle-aged man, Henry finally settled in England, in Rye's Lamb House. He adored his seaside cottage, but for many years it was merely a charming, weathered asylum; a sanctuary for the authorial enterprise. His true abode was great literature, what he called "one of the most elevating experiences within the reach of the human mind". The articulate wanderer found an enduring residence in his work.

And so did his friend, Miss Constance Fenimore Woolson – she called his writing "my true country, my real home". But she was no sycophantic fan. Constance was intelligent, fiercely independent and genuinely gifted. In an age when the bonds of patriarchy were only slowly loosening, Woolson was lauded as a fine novelist, poet and author of short-fiction and travelogues. And while her reputation is dim beside that of Henry James, she is still remembered for her rich portraits of the Great Lakes of North America. Like James, she was a wandering expatriate, vigilantly defending her privacy and freedom to write. And like him, Constance discovered a sanctuary in literature – in his art, alongside her own. They exchanged professional judgements, Woolson sometimes challenging James's mastery. For example, she asked the demiurge of Isabel Archer and Daisy Miller to be more ambitious with his heroines. "Why not," she asked, "give us a woman for whom we can feel real love?" If James responded with his characteristic silence, brevity or evasion, Woolson's candour was no less impressive: it was the honesty of a sincere, well-respected friend.

Both Henry and Constance were fastidious, reserved, solitary artists – gregarious in their way, but fearful of impropriety, interruption and cumbersome dependence. Accordingly, their friendship was a slow, tentative dance of proximity and distance. Despite his ongoing Platonic relationship with Miss Woolson, James seldom mentioned her to his family and close correspondents. And when he did, he admitted no affection and intimacy. He loved her in his way, but he wanted to keep this private, enclosed, sealed up. Colm Toibin, in his novel *The Master*, a fictionalized portrait of James's life, wrote of Woolson as James's "steadfast and self-contained and secret best friend". In their European holidays together, James and Woolson both revealed this ambivalence: separate floors in her Italian villa, separate houses in England, separate mornings and evenings of work. They wanted to be together but to preserve their independence for work. Alongside this professional distance was a kind of unhurried, non-intrusive tact. "Neither of them spoke," wrote Toibin, "about their private lives, their hidden selves." This wasn't a Romantic union of souls, a marriage of true minds consecrated by art. But it was a sincere, mature companionship: at once tender and aloof, tip-toeing between embrace and flight. It was as genuine a friendship as either had known.

A death in Venice

It ended tragically – with Woolson's violent, dramatic death. After many years in European orbit of one another, Henry and Constance were apart for the winter of 1893. Exhausted and psychologically spent after finishing her novel, Constance left England for Italy. Henry stayed in London, where he was "far from the maddening crowd, beside these sordid sands". An Italian holiday gives the impression of carefree, exotic repose. But this was a dangerous time for the authoress – she was lonely and prone to melancholy. She consoled herself with the prospect of Henry's next visit, writing to his sister-in-law, Alice James: "Mr. James will come to Italy every year." And more importantly, it seems their professional relationship was growing closer still. "Perhaps," she continued to Alice James, "we can write that play after all." However reassuring, this was a surprising admission. Henry James was a notoriously solitary artist. "He would have regarded collaboration," wrote his biographer Leon

Edel, "as an abandoning of sovereign ground." If he had shown a willingness to collaborate, this was a rare chance. More astonishingly still, Henry even gave the impression – perhaps accidentally, perhaps not – that he wanted a little condominium or townhouse with Constance; his precious Italian pied-à-terre. For months, it seemed that Miss Fenimore Woolson and Mr James would make a life together. It would never have been a marriage in any conventional sense – James was probably gay, in orientation if not in deed. (He saw spouses as "complicated and complicating appendages".) For Constance, though, it was the promise of happiness, an end to restive wandering and the ache of another grey, lonely winter.

But Henry never joined her in Florence or Venice. Perhaps his terror of intimacy reasserted itself; perhaps he knew he would be bad company. Either way, he retreated to Ramsgate in London, where the inhospitable weather left him free from interruptions. When he read that Constance was looking for a home on his behalf, he was quick to deny it. "I expressed myself clumsily to Miss Woolson," he told their mutual acquaintance, "in appearing to intimate that I was coming there to 'live'. I can only ... live in London." And that was the end of the matter. He knew Miss Woolson's ennui would grow in the Venetian winter, with no manuscript to occupy her mind. He knew she would be anxious, exhausted and alone. But he simply couldn't go – his quiet London study was too alluring. By January the next year, Constance was dead, broken by a fall from a second-storey window.

When Henry received the telegram of her death, he was undoubtedly shattered. And when suicide was suggested by the Venetian newspapers, he fell apart. "I have utterly collapsed," he wrote to his friend John Hay. "I have let everything go." He had lost his "gentlest and tenderest" friend, one of the few to permeate his thick skin. And adding to his distress, Henry felt guilty – worried that he had killed her with his casual remoteness and half-uttered promises. He wrote to friends, trying to convince them and himself that she was the victim of a "definite, irresponsible, delirious insanity". For him, delusional madness was better than a cool-headed goodbye to solitude and sadness. In this state of grief and shame, Henry was paralysed and he reverted to his customary seclusion. "Venice is not a place I want *immediately* to see," he wrote in a pained letter to Constance's friend, Katrina Bronson. "So I have kept away from you." He left for Italy two months later, in March.

As Constance's literary executor in Venice, James was confronted with an onerous task: to face the ghost of his dear friend, lingering among her furniture, old clothes and unpublished papers. ("Poor isolated and fundamentally tragic being!") But it didn't take long for Henry to crave his beloved solitude, with the comforting smell of ink and paper. He complained about the tourists in Venice, burdening him in their thousands; about the "copious aid and comfort" he gave Woolson's sister; about the "interruptions, distractions, and defeats" that accompanied his weeks in Venice with Constance's family. "The last six weeks," he wrote in his notebook, "have been a terrible sacrifice to the Moloch of one's endless personal social relations." And perhaps most tellingly, he lamented what he called "extended exposures": the horrifying possibility that his letters to Constance might be discovered and published. With his executor's authority, he took the many epistles she had kept and quietly disposed of them – some by fire, and some in the dark water of the Venetian lagoon. Woolson's estate finished with, he was soon back to work in his own apartment, Casa Biondetti.

It's understandable that the great author wanted to write, even in Venice – it was his life's calling. We can also appreciate James's concerns about privacy. Few of us would want our letters, conversations or emails broadcast for the world. But what is curious is the timing: even in the midst of his intense grief and guilt, Henry was retreating to the hermetic silence of the study. And perhaps more importantly, it was only in his "workshop" that he could repossess his friend. Woolson seemed to penetrate his consciousness more fully in death, as a literary inspiration, than in life. As his biographer Leon Edel suggests, this was the *idée fixe* of James's private life. "The Henry James who had difficulty in establishing full and charming connections with people in life," wrote Edel, "could do so when they were dead and locked within the crystal walls of his imagination." At the heart of his legendary reserve and prodigious oeuvre was a subtle, shifting, quiet retreat. Henry was a genius at sketching portraits of the psyche and its relationships – this is incontestable. But occasionally in life he sought distractions from this very thing.

With so much recent literature exploring the Jamesian myth, it's important not to adhere to a caricature of the great novelist. Henry James was by no means anti-social or sullen. On the contrary, he was famously gregarious, dining with the finest artists, authors and "civilized" families in all of Europe and America. He enjoyed company immensely, hence his now-legendary hundred-plus dinner invitations in a single London season. And for some – from Ivan Turgenev to Edith Wharton and his nephews and nieces – James was a tender, enduring intimate. "We all live together," he wrote to Grace Norton, "and those of us who love and know, live so most. We help each other – even unconsciously, each in our own effort, we lighten the effort of others." In his generosity, his attempts at consolation and his loyalty, James was a good friend, brother and son.

But James's sociability makes his tendency towards flight all the more intriguing. For all his gregariousness and prolific letter-writing, there was often something held back – "something incommunicable, something reserved", as Virginia Woolf put it. For the greater part of his life, even as he sought out "society", Henry feared the "Moloch" that stole his hours.

Significantly, this reveals more than the biographical minutiae of a great author. It suggests, with arresting clarity, the subtle threat at the heart of our battles with distraction: that attention to ourselves, or our private pursuits, often involves sacrificing our intimate relationships. Never completely, and rarely consciously, of course – but a quiet retreat occurs, often from those we are most lovingly entangled with. And perhaps more importantly, this isn't simply impressed upon us by circumstances. Our own predispositions and proclivities can encourage us to withdraw; can urge us to seek our own company, instead of the precariousness of love. We're not simply habituated by repetition but somehow primed by our makeup to turn inward, and enjoy the rewards of solitude and distance. In this, Henry James isn't a one-dimensional cautionary tale. His life cannot be reduced to one tragic scene, or single, compromising tendency. Instead, his struggles with privacy and reserve indicate a more common human drama: a fundamental, often unavoidable vacillation between self and other, I and Thou, proximity and safe distance. Like Matisse with his art and Bakunin with his politics, our most cherished objects of attention can blind us to closer, perhaps more nuanced, realities. In our devotion to work, art and public life, particularly when these are rewarding and recognized, we can be quietly distracted from one another.

Dear, dear, dearest …

But if this drama is common and deeply entrenched, it is by no means inexorable. Towards the end of his life, a different Henry James emerged. Whatever grew in the chrysalis of Lamb House was not a radically different beast; it was the same man, with shifted priorities. His fear of intimacy dissipated, his passions rose to the surface, and intensely so. The older author was just as ironic, cutting, analytic – but he became warmer and more openly affectionate. "The frigid wall of his egotism had been breached," wrote Leon Edel, "to an enlarged vision of the world, and a larger feeling of the world's human warmth."

And this wasn't unconscious or purely instinctive – James lucidly, patiently articulated his discovery. Less than three years before he died, he wrote to his friend Hugh Walpole. Walpole was a young man at the time – eager, energetic and charming to Henry. If James was critical of his friend's work, he enjoyed his company, addressing him fondly as "dearest, dearest, darlingest Hugh". But having committed to this, there was none of James's earlier hesitation; no backpedalling or retreating. He was straightforward, tender and unashamed. "I think I don't regret a single 'excess' of my responsive youth," he candidly explained, "I only regret, in my chilled age, certain occasions and possibilities I didn't embrace."

As this suggests, Henry's newfound clarity wasn't confined to Walpole, nor was it an unthinking switch. It was a more general thawing, conscious and perhaps even savoured. James, the master of cold literary form ("Morality is hot," he wrote to Violet Paget, "art is icy!"), was daring to commit more fully to the warmth of human relations. The most ardent of his letters in this vein were to Hendrik Anderson, a young American sculptor of Norwegian birth. In 1902, for example, Henry wrote to Hendrik in a spirit of consolation – the artist's older brother had just died, and Henry tried to sooth his grief in print, from across the Atlantic. "My dear, dear, dearest Hendrik," he wrote from Pall Mall, "your news fills me with horror and pity, and how can I express the tenderness with which it makes me think of you and the aching wish to be near you and put my arms around you?" Again and again, Henry tried to pour out his heart to Hendrik, as a salve for the young man's wounds. He invited him to Rye, and asked him to accept his intimate comforts. "Sooner or later to have you there," wrote the novelist as he neared sixty, "to put my arm around you and make you lean on me as a brother and a lover." This wasn't professional advice, or another business epistle. James wasn't running from Hendrik to the safety and predictability of work – on the contrary. He was undertaking one of the great risks of personal life: writing a love letter.

Of course, James had lost none of his critical faculty – he wasn't blinded by passion. If he begged Hendrik for his company ("Don't

... oh don't, pass me – on the wide waters."), he was also an austere critic. When the exuberant young sculptor told Henry of his plans for a "world city", the author was aghast. Hendrik wanted to erect a grand metropolis with squares and public fountains, which would promote happiness, peace and love. He enlisted the aid of the rich and well connected across Europe and the United States, all impressed by his bold vision and irrepressible spirit. James also admired Hendrik's passion and *joie de vivre*, but he thought his "cosmopolis" to be hubris. "The dread delusion to warn you against," he wrote in 1912, "is called in Medical Science MEGALO-MANIA (look it up in the dictionary!) ... the infatuated and disproportionate love and pursuit of ... the Big, the Bigger, the Biggest, the Immensest Immensity." But even in the midst of this sharp criticism and mockery, James was trying to demonstrate his affection. Instead of ending with a stern rebuke, Henry closed with parental tenderness. "Realize how dismally unspeakably much," he wrote, "these cold hard, desperate words, withholding sympathy, cost your ever-affectionate, your terribly tender old friend."

Perhaps it's no coincidence that these missives were intended for young men: Anderson, Walpole, Howard Sturgis, Jocelyn Persse. The middle-aged bachelor, alone in his seaside home, was hardly a ladies' man; he had no wife, no children, and no illicit mistress. A century on, it's certainly easy to see James as a closet homosexual, preferring Hendrik Anderson's "magnificent stature" to Miss Woolson's feminine charms. It's true that James displayed an ardent affection for young Hendrik, and adored Jocelyn Persse ("Henry James was madly in love with him," wrote Walpole). And James's friends Mary Duclaux and Urbain Mengin certainly discussed his mysterious sexuality; his willingness to "submit" to another man. Clearly his gender preferences were "unorthodox" enough to be a conversation piece. Perhaps his flight from Constance was that of an "invert" (in the terminology of the day), shrinking from the wrong sexual object.

But this is all a little too neat – a false clarity, achieved by modern sexual classifications. The resident of his "little old celibatoirean oak-parlour" might have enjoyed the company of young men, and made this known as he aged. But his expressions of fondness were never "sexual" in any straightforward sense. James deplored Oscar Wilde's ostentation (an "unclean beast", he said), and retained an abhorrence of *any* carnality – for himself, at least. "HJ submitting himself ... to such customs," wrote Mengin to Duclaux, "it's like trying to imagine you, Mary ... giving yourself a shot of heroin." More importantly, the warmth that emanated from the older Henry James was, if not more "pure", then more generous – it was a more ardent desire for *all* who mattered. This was the gregarious Master, the hospitable Uncle Henry, who gripped friends' arms tightly, or enveloped his nieces and nephews in hugs. "What I do want," he wrote to his sister-in-law, Alice, "is to personally and firmly and intimately encircle Peg and Aleck and their Mother and squeeze them as hard together as is compatible with squeezing them so tenderly." This expansion of familiarity was more than the discovery of a dormant homosexuality – it was a *glasnost* of the soul. The man who once cautiously, tentatively sought distraction from intimacy was now doing the opposite: giving *all* his loved ones sustained, intense, unashamed attention. He allowed life to touch him, without retreating to the safety of art.

At the same time, James's fiction also involved more intimacy – cerebral and physical. In *The Golden Bowl*, for example, the American heiress Maggie Verver is betrayed by her European, aristocratic husband. She is all innocence, naïveté, simplicity – and in her love for her father she alienates her groom. He woos her friend Charlotte, the father's young bride. Instead of being crushed, Maggie develops worldly maturity. She sends her father overseas, along with Charlotte – her friend gets to keep her money and lifestyle but loses her lover. Maggie keeps her prince, who is now the husband of a sophisticated, strong, *knowing* young woman. James's denouement involves a disarming honesty about sexual attraction, gender roles and power: a very modern recognition of mind and society, their cracks and potholes. In the same way, *The Ambassadors* confronts deceit and sexual freedom with literary confidence. The hero, poor Lambert Strether, finds himself celebrating French licence, perhaps the very "occasions and possibilities" James himself regretted abjuring. Even *The Portrait of a Lady*, the archetypal novel of retreat, was rewritten to include raw human passion. In the definitive New York edition, a single line describing a kiss became a stunning evocation of passion and its consequence. "His kiss was like white lightning," wrote the Master, "a flash that spread, and spread again, and stayed; and ... she felt each thing in his hard manhood that had least pleased her, each aggressive fact of his face, his figure, his presence." In this way, James's last novels and short stories were still indirect, subtle and genteel, but they were unflinching: unafraid to give the murky world of love and attraction their attention. In their portraits of shifting, elusive, situated selves, they exemplified fidelity, not diversion or deceit.

Henry James's epiphany was thus a kind of lived harmony: between life and art, truth and illusion, worldliness and innocence. This was partly a reconciliation between two Henry Jameses: the Yankee and the Continental. He longed for refined European rites and rituals – the "barnacles of old Europe" his brother saw on him. He enjoyed elegance, etiquette, charm; the manners of the salon. But at the same time, he saw the hollowness of this: the cruelty, manipulation and *Schadenfreude* behind the polished screen. As an American, and, in many ways, a Puritan, Henry was unsettled by the façade that obscured reactionary, un-egalitarian, bigoted Europe. If he deplored cloying innocence, he also loathed baseness and vulgarity – the vices hidden by ancient "breeding". These international conflicts were part of a more metaphysical struggle: between a life of contrivance and intellectual sovereignty, and one of passion, vulnerability and disappointment. If James, as the consummate artist, affirmed illusion, it was knowingly. He chose to forge his own world of semblance, without the comfort of believing it real.

And at the same time, James embraced life and love, unvarnished by convenient fictions. The sexagenarian magician sought art *and* life, and no longer used the former as a diversion from the pains of the latter. His instinct for intimacy was fused, finally and confidently, with the creative impulse. The result was a more attuned, less distracted, consciousness – a perception unafraid to take in the world of others, and intertwine it honestly with his craft. At the end of his years, James embodied what he had once aphorized as a critic: "art without life is a poor affair".

James on James

A suggestive explanation of Henry James's struggles comes from his brother, William "Bill" James. The eminent psychologist and philosopher never diagnosed his "Harry" in any straightforward way. And in many ways, William was blinded by familiarity, by the jaundiced eye of the disapproving big brother. Nonetheless, William's insightful and grounded writings offer an intriguing account of Henry James's Damascus transformation. They suggest that Harry was battling quite common anxieties and longings, that the desire for distractions from intimacy is normal and, more importantly, something we can all overcome.

In his textbook *The Principles of Psychology*, William devoted a long passage to the human instincts. He wanted to clarify which impulses and urges came naturally, and how and why they were dammed up. Alongside fear, imitation and play, William listed the most obvious urge of all: love. By this, he meant chiefly the sexual instinct, but also the need for company, intimacy, society.

The professor noted that this instinct is often seen as simple and irrepressible – "blind, automatic, and untaught", as he put it. And certainly, it is an intense and often unconscious force in civilization. But William was quick to correct this one-sided view. The instincts of love and procreation aren't sovereign; we don't spend every waking hour making friends or whoopee. "The sexual instinct," he wrote, "is particularly liable to be checked and modified by slight differences in the individual stimulus, by the inward condition of the agent himself, by habits once acquired, and by the antagonisms of contrary impulses operating as the mind." Put simply, the sex drive is undoubtedly ubiquitous and intense. But it isn't omnipotent. Instead, it is always held back by equally powerful instincts, which play "a vital part in the amelioration of all higher animal types".

In particular, James identified what he called "the anti-sexual instinct": a spontaneous and unthinking retreat from intimacy. He wrote of the disgust we have sitting in a chair warmed by a stranger, and the loathing of shaking hands. It can be such a formidable barrier to intimacy that some people *never* find love. Violent though the sexual instinct is, wrote James, "individuals in whom the inhibiting influences are potent may pass through life and never find an occasion to have it gratified". The instinct merges with shyness, modesty, chastity and the gamut of privative character traits to imprison a psyche within itself.

Obviously, we needn't accept this philosophy as gospel. It contains more than a grain of Puritan psychology, with its disparaging attitude to sex (he didn't like Freud's lectures on dreams). It's difficult to believe there is a specific instinct against intercourse and procreation, even if the consequences are guilt or celibacy. More likely is a more general discomfort with intimacy; a withdrawal from closeness, physical or mental. The origin of this is as basic as the professor supposed: it lies in our urge to protect ourselves and to maintain and regulate our boundaries. In the vulnerable nerves of unseen viscera, and the equally enigmatic maze of our psyche, there is more than enough motive for this. Our mind, as much as our skin, seeks to enforce its barriers. In fact, this is one of the very definitions of an organism – if living things are affected, permeable, changeable, they are also discrete and contained; they work hard to protect their vital insides and maintain their commodious shape. "Each mind," wrote William James, "must have a certain minimum of selfishness in the shape of instincts of bodily self-seeking in order to exist." And we might add that it's not only the body that is sought – it's the entire ensemble of identity, flesh and spirit. What James called the "anti-sexual instinct" is simply one version of this – just as primal as a snail's retracted antennae, or the curling-up of a woodlouse. In situations of perceived danger, stress or pain, even if mistakenly amplified by our own sensitivities, we withdraw. And the more often this occurs, the more insistently it forms habits. In this, what begins as raw, uncultured drive is incorporated into the variegated biases we call the self. The sudden flinch is transformed from reflex to custom. Despite William's emphasis, this goes beyond sex, encompassing the span of human relations; it's what might be called a solitary impulse.

Importantly, William James wasn't referring directly to Henry in these theories. To be sure, he *did* see his little brother as "at bottom very powerless-feeling"; as a weak, insular, perhaps superficial Europhile. And no doubt his Henry, his mother's "angel", fell into habits of passivity, lethargy and illness with William around. "The Angel and his brother," wrote Leon Edel, "could not long remain in each other's company without experiencing a certain amount of physical, and moral discomfort."

But William was being candid about his *own* shortcomings. If there were an "anti-sexual instinct", and its equivalent in everyday intimacy, the scholar thought he himself exemplified it. Before he married, William was inexperienced, ashamed and hopeless – he thought he would never find love. At the age of thirty-four, he yearned for the fulfilment of marriage: carnal, social, spiritual. But he was beset by doubts, and he automatically recoiled at familiarity. While his friend Alice Gibbens was straightforward and affectionate, her beau swung between romantic ardour and anxious retreat. In every bit of praise and charm Alice evoked, William saw flaw, defect, vice. "I will suppose you feel a sympathy with me," he wrote to her in 1876, "but I can furnish you with undreamt of arguments *against* accepting any offer I may make." William was torn between two fundamental, pervasive instincts: insularity and a desire to be known, understood.

Obviously, there is more than an echo of Henry James's troubles in William's struggle. The tension between inwardness and affection William experienced with Alice was mirrored by Harry's own conflict: closeness and privacy, society and solitude, a life of vulnerability and the impenetrable fortress of art. William saw glimpses of New England Puritanism in this, oppressing generations of young men and women with fragile, paralysed sensibility – "making us say retire instead of go to bed, and forbidding us to call a female dog by name". But as a scientist, William identified more basic drives at work; fundamental tendencies to offer or withhold, advance or retreat, touch or avoid. If these were heightened in Boston or Newport, they were present in *all* societies, from the naked Brazilian girls of William's anthropological studies, to the aristocrats of Henry's Continental visits. And they are with us today (but more of this later).

In light of William's ideas, Henry James's *glasnost* was more than a matter of cerebral shifts, crucial as these are. It was the careful domestication of two opposing instincts and their psychological and social complements. And to achieve this in a lasting, enduring fashion, Henry had to claim the very thing he gave his Maggie Ververs and Isabel Archers, even if they lost it: freedom.

The moment of freedom

As a *scientist*, William couldn't speak of freedom. Psychology was the study of natural processes: laws, rules, principles. They involved iron-clad necessities, which brooked no deviation. For this reason, "the question of free-will," he wrote in *Principles of Psychology*, "is insoluble on strictly psychological grounds." He didn't mean that freedom was a chimera, a fantasy of otherwise shackled minds. Instead, his point was that, whatever freedom was, it couldn't be reduced to the simple cause and effect of atoms or chemicals. "Science ... must be constantly reminded," he continued, "that her purposes are not the only purposes." If we want to grasp the nettle of liberty, we have to set aside the logic of science and turn to the "inner life" of the emancipated mind.

William gave an inspiring portrait of freedom in an address to the Harvard divinity students, later published as "The Dilemma of Determinism". It wasn't a complete theory of liberty – more a heartfelt but lucid investigation of the moment of freedom: the instant we reclaim our self-possession. As a man who had long struggled with bodily exhaustion and spiritual lethargy, the professor took freedom seriously – it was a "gift", he said. And because of this, he didn't want to do a slipshod job. He endeavoured to unflinchingly think through a world without liberty; a world where everything *must* be and can't be otherwise. He sketched out, in straightforward, clear prose, the cosmos of the so-called "determinists". And along the way, he touched on his own quietism, voyeurism and flight – and that of his brother, Henry.

For many in William's day, the world was one of definite and unalterable fate. Whatever happened was *always* going to do so, from the beginning of the cosmos to the end. Every bit of the universe was like a prisoner shackled in a chain gang – each was tightly tied to the movements and momentum of the other. It was a world of absolute necessity – what the professor called "one unbending unit of fact". Of course, the teachers and butchers, coal miners and chemists of nineteenth-century America weren't this philosophically articulate or systematic. They weren't scientists or engineers. But like many of us today, they had this portrait in the back of their minds: a vision of a universe where everything was already decreed, planned, commanded. As we saw earlier, this was the very Puritan cosmos that flourished in England and New England (including Harvard, where William was speaking) and which spread widely with capitalism. It involved the sway of what Weber called "predestination", as well as the transformation of the world into a machine of calculated necessities.

At its least "philosophical" and most prosaic, this was a habitual and widespread deference to what is: to the fixity of given reality. It was associated not only with conservatism and traditional mores but also with a certain failure of imagination: to envisage possibilities, potentials, opportunities – other than those of the status quo. It was a training in acceptance and often promotion of perceived reality and an unwillingness to question what might otherwise be (or become).

As this suggests, what was missing from this cosmos, Professor James told his religious students, was "chance". Not randomness or chaos, but a little looseness, room to move, plasticity. For him, chance didn't mean doing anything or everything – it simply meant you didn't have to think, move and speak with the rest of the chain gang. Put simply, the determinists' world was missing possibility: that something *might* be, but needn't be. In this chance universe (which William thought was ours), "actualities seem to float in a sea of possibilities". A world without this ocean of chance is one without freedom.

William James found this over-determined, constraining world terrifying, but he investigated it soberly. He looked at its very real consequences – and he didn't like them one bit. If we're deprived of liberty, we *can* act in good faith (like the finest Puritans), but we very often retreat into the kingdom of ourselves. We fall back on what the professor called "subjectivism". In the face of the world's utter indifference, we console ourselves with knowledge and sensibility. Many Protestants, for example, saw God's universe as an immutable law – their worldly deeds were impotent and they disintegrated before fact. But these people had wisdom: all the sins of the world taught them God's lessons. They steeled themselves to war, famine, poverty and petty barbarisms, all in the name of divine insight – not to *do* anything, but simply to *know*. Weaker, more fragile souls lapsed into hedonism or voyeurism: they simply stood back and watched, or they wallowed in sensation and perception. In both cases, the universe was unwaveringly evil, but it fuelled our psyche. "Admirable artifice of nature!" said William, "in order the better to enlighten us." The tendency was to hide, withdraw, flinch: to be observers instead of participants.

There was more than a touch of this in Professor James as a young man – and also in Henry. The little brother often hung back, stood and watched, took notes. Though he retreated from intimacy, Henry was a keen observer. ("Tell me what the artist is," he wrote, "and I shall tell you of what he has been conscious.") In his memoirs, the great author wrote of his time as a child, when William would "play with boys who curse and swear" while he hung back, "gaping". In this, he embodied the "subjectivism" of William's philosophy: seeking knowledge, in the tragedy around him, and the sensory rewards of tourism and distant inspection. In an early essay on the Russian novelist Turgenev, Henry expressed this philosophy lucidly. "The world as it stands," he wrote, "is no illusion, no phantasm, no evil dream of a night; we can neither forget it, not deny it, nor dispense with it. We can welcome experience as it comes, and give it what it demands, in exchange for something ... which contributes to swell the volume of consciousness." As this suggests, young Henry was enriched by the pageant of perception, but he didn't think that he could act. His counsel was always to hold back, be patient, withhold action. "Don't think, don't feel ... don't conclude or decide," he wrote to his friend Grace Norton, "don't do anything but *wait*."

For William James, this was precisely how the soul retired in a cosmos of unalterable fact. If there was a basic solitary impulse, it was perfectly adapted to this world and was regulated accordingly: with retreat, flight and withdrawal. This is what William called "the fatalistic mood of mind". And, in their moments of crisis or worry, it was leaving both brothers (despite their genius, reputation and "society") prey to melancholy and isolation.

To overcome this "inward remedilessness", as William described it, humanity had to accept possibility, indeterminacy, singularity – and accept the enterprise of freedom. The secret of this freedom, as he saw it, was perhaps too radical and too commonplace for philosophy. "Our first act of freedom, if we are free," the professor told the divinity students, "ought in all inward propriety to be to affirm that we are free." The genesis of personal freedom was the very acknowledgement of it.

For William, this meant a decisive break with inwardness, a refusal to obey the solitary impulse. "In the beginning was the Deed," said Goethe's Faust, and Professor James agreed. As a younger man beset by depression, he had recognized this. "I may not study, make, or enjoy," he wrote bleakly in his journal, "but I can will." In reply to a world that seems inexorable, unbending, we must act, he said – grasp good luck, seize opportunity, and, perhaps most crucially, reach out to one another. And standing before New England's future theologians and ministers, he affirmed this in sparse, elegant theory. "No matter how we succeed in doing our outward duties," he told the students, "whether gladly or spontaneously, or heavily and unwillingly, do them we somehow must; for the leaving of them undone is perdition." And the motive for this was a simple one: guilt, regret, shame, and the host of emotions that accompany failure and frustration. It was the "occasions and possibilities"

Henry wrote of to Hugh Walpole, and his nagging feeling of lost opportunity. For William, this otherwise paralysing mood was the key to liberty. If we can regret, then we admit that things could have once been otherwise. And if this is so, then perhaps *we* could make them otherwise. "I cannot understand regret," he said, "without the admission of real, genuine possibilities in the world." The instant we bemoan our mistakes – and slander the universe – in that very same moment we endorse our freedom.

For William, the next step was one of keen, enduring attention. "Effort of attention," wrote the professor, "is the essential phenomenon of will." More particularly, liberty requires attention to ideas. In his *Principles of Psychology*, William argued that *all* our voluntary movements are motivated by ideas. We can walk the dog, eat dinner and do household chores out of habit, but genuinely free deeds are inspired by ideas: representations, impressions, conceptions. Even the most abstract, formal idea motivates some movement – even if it's a sigh, a blink or a breath. When we don't move, it's often because we have too many ideas: our attention is divided, weakened, fragmented, and our psyche is paralysed. To act decisively and diligently, we have to clear away conflicting, contrary ideas – what William called "murdering the vanquished possibility". And for the professor, this was why the *idea* of freedom was so important. Having grasped the ideal of liberty, our chief task is to hold to it fast, banish obscuring thoughts, and allow our ideas to inspire movement, action, deeds. Put simply, distraction and diversion, as I've suggested in this book, are the enemy of freedom.

This might seem like a piece of sophistry; philosophical conjurer's trick, that avoids the dense metaphysical detail of freedom itself. And perhaps, as a pragmatist, William James sidestepped many of the common debates among his scholarly fraternity. But it remains a genuinely innovative and ultimately quite practical assessment of the relationship between ideas, freedom and distraction. More specifically, it holds fast to the simple, incontrovertible truth: if we are free with our attention and intellect, then the prize of freedom is gained by nothing other than the assertion of this fact. It encourages us, even in the midst of constraints and doubts, to take responsibility for our own experience; to feel, think and act, instead of waiting for the world to turn out as we might wish. And most crucially, it's a reminder of the unique, precious event that is human connection: two people freely and knowingly adhering to one another, when they could tragically, lamentably, *not*.

This challenge was what confronted Henry James as he sat in Lamb House – often alone, but for his dachshund Max, that "precious little person". He could bow to the instincts of inwardness and to polite traditions of modesty and shyness, or he could seek engagement with the world and its dear inhabitants. He could use art as a convenient diversion from the trials and rewards of intimacy, or he could incorporate it into life. To begin this, Henry had to claim his liberty: that first, final resolve to *do*, and do so with his own law, his own necessity. And then he had to hold fast to this ideal and not allow it to diminish or dissolve – "the resolute effort of attention", as William described it.

Henry already had a glimpse of this endeavour in his lonely vocation, what he called "driving the pen". In the laborious, careful weaving of idea and sensation, and the precise selection and combination of words, passages – in *this* he knew his will. He was familiar with its sovereignty: the "I" that demanded, recreated, ordered and possessed. And Harry recognized this in his brother's philosophy. "I'm *with* you, all along the line," he wrote to William in 1909, after reading *A Pluralistic Universe*. "As an artist & a 'creator' I can catch on, hold on, to pragmatism." In the inner world of fiction, he understood the vital fiat of will and the singularity of the individual.

But Henry had to achieve this in life, and alongside others: different psyches, with all their prickly idiosyncrasies. It would mean pain, privation, frustration and awkwardness – it was a violation of his literary carapace, his Continental barnacles. Still, time was running out, and the moment to *do* was upon him. Unlike his brother the renowned "psychic researcher", Henry never expected life after death. He liked to believe, he told an audience in 1907, that a profound, lively, intense consciousness warranted immortality; that anything else would be a tease, a mockery, a cruel taunt. But he stressed the "like", because he had no faith in a posthumous life. He saw all around him "the relentless ebb of the tide" and knew his days were numbered. His "poor palpable, ponderable, probeable, laboratory-brain" was slowly decaying – and taking him with it. If he desired immortality for his rare and precious spirit, he couldn't rely on it. And so Henry had to expand, enrich, diversify his adoration for living, in case his soul was snuffed out.

Spurred by this *memento mori*, perhaps his brother's words on freedom rang in his ears. "The issue is decided," William counselled, "nowhere else than the *here* and *now*." Stung by nagging regret, and conscious of his mortality, Henry undertook what William called "the outward act". He did precisely what his brother – in a more considerate, generous mood – would have recommended. Harry sketched out, in delicate, throbbing prose, the vicissitudes of love; its falsities, surprises, gifts. He depicted loss and discovery, and ceased to shy away from the magnesium white of passion. He presented his protagonists with the knowledge born of sacrifice – to live, to love, to commit without timid reservations. In doing so, he told himself what Strether told Bilham in *The Ambassadors*. "Do what you like," said the amiable New Englander, "so long as you don't make my mistake. For it was a mistake. Live!" This, in his rhythmic, surprisingly forthright way, was Henry James clearing the fog of conflicting concepts and fixing on a motivating impression: a life of sincere, reserved but genuine passion, shared with beloved friends. As articulated in *The Ambassadors* and his other later works, this was the great liberating idea, one that spurred the ageing Master to newfound intimacy. Armed with his sublime literary portraits, he held firmly to ideas of friendship, companionship, love. Despite lingering illness, ongoing tragedy and the demands of his vocation, he wasn't waylaid. He kept his loved ones firmly in his mind, and the ideas led to action. Instead of being paralysed, he reached out: in letters, lunches and embraces. ("Feel, feel, I say," he wrote in one letter, "feel for all your worth, and even if it half kills you, for that is the only way to live.") Giving his love freely, he was rewarded with a measure of happiness. Of course this was a truism – but it was a truism Henry James had to live for himself.

The point of this isn't a Platonic one: that art diminishes life and threatens reason. Henry James exemplifies no intrinsic conflict between creation and fact. Instead, the Master suggests an enduring tension in the human condition: between advance and retreat, intimacy and solitude, social attention and the inner life of the individual. In James's case – and, to some extent, in his brother's also – art was the splendid realization of all his powers. It "made his life", to paraphrase the author. But because of its distinctive rewards, psychological and monetary, it also offered Henry a convenient and justifiable retreat from the threatening presence of others. It afforded the perfect distraction from intimacy, a private realm where his will was sovereign. Yet it could have been butchery, chemistry or philosophy; it could have been gambling or sport. Literature allowed a very particular kind of asylum, but it shared with many professions and entertainments the virtue of alleviating his intense, instinctual fear of proximity, closeness.

What makes Henry James such a compelling, illuminating character isn't simply his uniqueness but his common labours; his battle with the lure of privative amusement, or casual indifference. While heightened by Puritanism and the customs of the Victorian age, Henry's solitary impulse was perfectly, consolingly human. And his struggles against indifference or flight involved the very same stakes we confront today: the achievement of a tangible, worldly freedom, through enduring, sympathetic attention to others.

The Jamesian today

There are many reasons for the current interest in Henry James. One, of course, is literary. As an influence on the "modern" sensibility, James is a fascinating progenitor of an age now dwindling (if we believe the pundits, that is). Indeed, as one of the innovators of the modern novel, James exemplifies a literary form now in question. Another reason for our curiosity is a mix of nostalgia and garden-variety willingness to be amused. As a wit, a "somebody" who dined with literary greats and heads of State, and as a citizen of a lost Victorian world, James invites attention. But James also remains fascinating as a voice of intriguing, enduring human drama. The life and writings of the wandering expatriate, born more than 150 years ago, still offer precious insights on our own struggles.

At a time when many of us are reporting diminished closeness – with friends, loved ones, family – the trials of James's literature and life can be strikingly familiar. Behind the Continental opacity, the Puritan reserve, the façade of starch and silence, is the same conflict between intimacy and solitude, inner life and society, commitment and vacillation. We read (and often reread, because sleep intervenes) Henry James because he presents, in elaborate, circuitous prose, timeless adventures in social distraction; in the turned face, the downward glance, the unspoken confession. (And more often than not, we read James in a quiet room, the stark silence perhaps softened by music; in bed, two nightlights illuminating separate, solitary worlds; in a café, where the imprecise murmur of the crowd gives us the peace his exquisite lines demand.) If we are touched by his *joie de vivre*, what Woolf called his "enormous, sustained, increasing, overwhelming love for life", we often obtain commerce with it alone – seeking in him a fellow refugee from company, while at the same time enriching our vision of human intimacy.

In many ways, these urges – for solitude, peace, our own company – are more common today than in James's time. Oddly, the digital age is Jamesian. This seems absurd in a period that offers so many opportunities for communication. As we've seen, modern contrivances afford rapid, incessant flows of information; they incorporate us, often with our consent, into a realm of necessity. But this is precisely why we might *want* to be left alone – we're shrinking before the "unbending unit of fact", as William James put it. This steady, nagging stream of data can make us, even more than Henry, retreat before the demands of society. Because we often don't have his luxury of time – weeks abroad, delays of surface mail, provincial houses without phones – we sometimes need to find reprieve in snatches. If we only have a few hours at our disposal before the digital connections of business reattach themselves, it makes sense to seek the instant relaxation of online browsing, text messages or half-listened phone calls while shopping, smoking, daydreaming. All these modes of easy telecommunication are preferable to the sharp, draining presence of another person in the room, particularly one that "matters". If we are to speak, to read of one another, telecommunications can offer the information without the intimacy – the disembodied voice or text lacks the imploring, perhaps violating presence of proximity. Put simply, technological life offers us both the aggravations of continual interaction, and the tools for distancing ourselves from it. In ways subtle and unperturbing, we can withdraw from intimacy without hanging up, logging off. At times, we want its cool necessity, because the realm of human immediacy – of imprecision, spontaneity, vulnerability, betrayal – can be harder to endure.

Perhaps the most common forum for this, though, is work itself, where so many of us spend our waking hours and productive years. We've seen what professional life offers: money, order, skills and – if used well – the priceless cache of free time. But it's also an asylum from intimate entanglements. Henry James's career offered very specific benefits for the rootless bachelor, rewards perhaps inaccessible to most of us. Yet it had in common with today's employment an acceptable and justifiable excuse for flight. On so many occasions, Henry didn't have to dampen his impulsive backward convulsion; the hackles raised by proximity. He simply deferred to the importance of work. Quite literally, work offers a legitimate and publicly esteemed distraction from the mental sediment of intimacy. This is perhaps the most wonderful virtue of the "workmate", the professional colleague. They afford collaboration, company, James's "society", without the baggage of home.

And perhaps it's wise to remember precisely *why* our intimates are who they are: because they are brilliantly, intrusively, sometimes painfully lodged in our psyche. "The most peculiar social self which we're apt to have," wrote William James, "is in the mind of the person one is in love with. The good and bad fortune of this self cause the most intense elation and dejection." They are so unshakably, extremely dear to us, but they are also sources of irritation, exhaustion and confusion. At work, we're allowed to divert ourselves from our loved ones; to forge functional, confident, perhaps even more likeable identities, unachievable in the ambivalent tangle of home life.

Friends offer us other opportunities for respite; safe ports for the rickety yacht of the soul. It might appear strange to see friends as alternatives to intimacy – surely they are, to paraphrase Aristotle, second selves, with all the consolations this implies? Certainly, our closest friends can be very much so, and sometimes more than blood relatives or spouses. This is precisely why so many of us are nursed through break-ups by friends: they are often the attentive, disinterested, loyal fonts of care we rely on in a crisis.

But friends can also be a burden – a source of obligation, duty, debt. For this reason, it's common to seek diversion in less demanding company. Our casual acquaintances allow for company, conversation and entertainment, without the sting of domestic routine and its sometimes overwhelming intimacies. Online friendships afford a similar bounty: instantaneous, often hilarious adventures in debate, discussion, dialogue. The ties are strong enough to sate the social urge, but their gossamer threads never bind us tightly, rarely ask for the commitments and cohabitations of our closest relationships. In all these cases, we repeat the struggles of Henry James, and every half-anxious, half-adoring ancestor, who fled the ambivalent treasury of intimacy. We might be using modern technologies and justifications, but the dilemma is ancient: to freely and knowingly confront another psyche, or to seek consoling distraction in a more palatable encounter.

In many ways, Henry James reveals how this dilemma is amplified in art. For art is a site for intense, vivid, enlivened perception; a realm where distraction is perhaps most obviously diagnosed and most disappointing. But in Henry's evasions and encounters, we can see art simultaneously as diversion and celebrant. It gives solitary souls the opportunity for seclusion, while also bringing people together – in print and in the commonwealth of ideas and impressions. As we saw earlier, art is as much asylum as provocation, is equally private sanctuary and public monument. Henry James reminds us that our beloved, comforting, sublime masterpieces can also serve as replacements for genuine human contact. And only a wilful, disciplined to and fro between life and its creative expression can achieve the balance that Henry belatedly, perhaps all too zealously achieved. To use art sensibly and effectively – and there's no other way to phrase it – requires and encourages a flexible, mindful liberty: one eye on our own brimming imagination and another on those precious minds we adore.

In every significant arena of life, this challenge appears: to seeks what is worthwhile, without narrowness, rigidity, bloody-minded deference to the status quo. If art offers enlivened experience, technology the chance of amplified potencies, politics the opportunity for cultivation – if each of these can be carefully employed to emancipate our characters – then there is also the possibility for inwardness and the sacrificial rite of social severance.

But a more intense, adoring, receptive existence needn't be purchased at the cost of intimacy – this is the implication of Henry James's fraught, mannered, endearingly tender familiarity. It requires a willingness to admit that sometimes, even with those we adore, we *want* to remain untouched, unimpinged, and an awareness that this can be mistaken, habitually unthinking and inadvertently painful. It means keeping one eye on our blind instincts and another on our ideals. But most crucially of all, it necessitates freedom: the clear and unwavering possession of liberty, and the willingness to safeguard it from the obscurity of conflicting conceptions – even when these are consecrated. It takes an imaginary leap into new impressions, whether wrought in fiction, blogs, conversations or the silent communion of the mind. This is Henry James's message from the grave: in the fight against distraction, intimacy – in all its astonishing incarnations – need not be a casualty.

7. Footnotes to Plato

> We are not gods, we are absurd limited beings, we live with affliction and chance. The most important things are close to us, the truth is close, in front of our noses.
> (Socrates to Plato, in Iris Murdoch's *Acastos*)

Alfred North Whitehead once referred to philosophy as "footnotes to Plato". Perhaps he was being a little facetious – but only a little. The tradition of Western philosophy is heavily indebted to the Athenian for its tone, topics and aspirations of worldly importance. And perhaps most impressively, Plato seemed to do away with so much froth and chatter – his was a single-minded, uncluttered vision of the cosmos. After so many centuries, Plato remains *the* touchstone of Western intellectual endeavour: you are either for or against him – indifference is almost unphilosophical.

But Plato's high-minded decisiveness is deceptive. In many ways, he exemplified distraction. Despite his virtues, the brilliant Athenian noble was in flight from life's earthly limitations. His abstractions, his universals, his denial of sex and flesh all suggest a flinch – a retreat in the face of life's sacrifices and compromises. Unable or unwilling to accept the fraught conditions of workaday reality, he sought solace in imaginary perfection. He fantasized about the Forms, a realm without pain, decay and death. And there is, as Schiller maintained, nothing wrong with imagination. But Plato did not let dreams be dreams – he transformed his phantasm into a hard fact. He lambasted the arts for their impurity and he denied what the Greeks were so impressively honest about: mortality. To my mind, this may be the most elegant, alluring error in our intellectual tradition: a profound no to life.

The point isn't that Plato was a villain or a fool – far from it. His chief vice was that he was, after all, a man. His grand metaphysical gambit was understandably human; it was both common and intelligible. Regardless of age, gender or station in life, we can *all* live as if death were unreal; as if the better part of ourselves were immortal and unlimited.

But this is the very heart of distraction: an inability to confront the basic situation of humanity. If our little life is "rounded with a sleep", then our waking hours will always be a struggle between competing, conflicting demands. Within these constraints, it's crucial that we make the right decisions, form the right habits, cultivate the right ideals. This is why Proust and Matisse were so infuriated by Law – it was wasting their faculties, denying their aspirations, obscuring the unique rewards they found in literature and art.

And this is precisely the significance of values: not Plato's immortal, ghostly figures but real-world preferences, tastes, distinctions. Values inform our judgements on what will most afford us insight, vitality, presence of mind and perhaps even happiness. They allow us to identify the best use of our dwindling or precious resources: time, energy, attention. Of course, we needn't all have the *same* standards – lucid, compelling values led Seneca to his retirement, and Eliot to his frantic, nervous professionalism. Though they suffered, each accepted his ailments in the name of his chosen ideals – he thought them worth living and dying for.

In an age of innumerable, intense diversions, we sometimes lack Eliot's discernment or Seneca's force of will. We develop the wrong values, or lose the wherewithal to apply them judiciously. This, as we've seen, is the ongoing struggle of a finite life. Out of either confusion, exhaustion or misplaced deference to vague ideals, we invest our resources badly, squandering them. The result is diminished wellbeing: we fail to enliven our psyche, cultivate our health, or realize our ambitions.

And as a rule, this encourages further oversights and slippages – a distracted mind is a clumsy, fumbling guide. But more importantly, the disappointment this breeds can compel us to flee more zealously; to seek asylum in false consolation, delusion or ubiquitous noise. Like poor Bakunin, haunted by a lifetime of blunders, we can sometimes seek consolation in egotism, self-delusion. In this sense, distraction can be a vicious cycle: it leads to disenchantment – precisely what we desire to be distracted from. Rather than seeking the equivalent of Spinoza's steadfast peace of mind, or Matisse's obstinate creativity, we take the path of Plato. This is what it means to be distracted: to retreat from ourselves and from the world we've mistakenly, sometimes hastily, embraced.

The opposite of distraction is a life of liberty – one spent not in seeking refuge from ourselves and the world but in sincerely taking up the challenge of existence; of "being" something rather than anything, in the time we have. We are all, as Heidegger cheerily put it, "dying already". If this is so, then there's little time to squander. This endeavour requires an honest, sometimes courageous recognition of what is life-affirming or inspiring, and the vigilance to safeguard this vision from corruption or misunderstanding. It entails the sobriety and patience of Mill, the profundity of Heidegger, the good humour of Nietzsche, the late tenderness of Henry James. And perhaps it even demands the imagination of Plato – without the alchemy that changes reverie into rock-hard reality.

But most crucially, an undistracted life requires gratitude. In Plato's *Phaedrus*, Socrates remarked that the destitute were the most grateful – to those who helped them, of course. The assumption is that gratitude is a kind of relief, the fondness we feel for a benefactor. The Greeks had a word for this, *charis*, and it was often the lot of slaves and supplicants – in other words, those without liberty.

Yet there is a more primordial, anonymous gratitude, not to a patron or a saviour but for the simple fact of existence itself. If we cannot choose our birth, or vault the impermeable barriers of place and time, we can still warm to the existential endeavour; we can smile at the opportunity to live, instead of flinching or closing our eyes. Of course this will entail pain and loss, sacrifice and compromise. And there will be time for games and idleness, for *Doctor Who* and songs in Arabic scales. But at its most profound, this is a simple, primal yes: to the attempt, the aspiration, the lurch towards freedom. To seek emancipation from distraction is to accept this ambivalent liberty – an unspoken, unrepentant thank you for the adventure of becoming.

8. Balancing the books

> The Bookstore, home of delights and haunt of fancy.
> (Henry James, *A Small Boy and Others*, 1913)

"Buying books would be a good thing," quipped Schopenhauer, "if one could also buy the time to read them in." In this, the misanthropic German revealed the dilemma for all book lovers: so many books, so little time. According to the US trade magazine *Publishers Weekly*, a quarter of a million books are published annually in the United States alone. Once you allow for language, genre, taste and luck, it's still possible to be intrigued or provoked by hundreds of titles every year. And then there are all the old books: from ancient works of Greek philosophy, Roman drama or Japanese religion, to last year's missed blockbuster. Unlike films or paintings, these works can't be enjoyed in an hour. We have to devote days and weeks to them. (This was the rationale behind T. S. Eliot's terse defence of poetry in the modern age: "It takes up less space.") Put simply, literature is yet another forum for distraction; a chance to be waylaid by less valuable pursuits.

With this in mind, I've written a few words on the more charming, profound or authoritative books and essays I've read for *Distraction*. Most titles are stocked in universities or public collections, but some are worth buying. A home library is a wonderful thing – it offers continuity, access and inspiration. Perhaps most importantly, it stands as an enduring emblem of our ambitions and experiences. And this is particularly so for books we've discovered in out-of-the-way second-hand shops. "Second hand books are wild books, homeless books," wrote Virginia Woolf, "they have come together in vast flocks of variegated feather, and have a charm which the domesticated volumes of the library lack." For this reason, I've also discussed editions, affordability and availability here and there. With (now) two small children at home, I don't have Woolf's free days to scour bookshops for prize finds. So, for online second-hand book-fossicking, I recommend http://www.abebooks.com – it lacks the spontaneity, sociability and adventure of bookshop browsing, but it is reliable and thrifty.

1. Manholes and tears

As a non-expert, I found Harold Pashler's *The Psychology of Attention* (Cambridge, MA: MIT Press, 1999) a concise introduction to the science of attention and distraction. Elizabeth Styles's *Attention, Perception and Memory: An Integrated Approach* (Hove: Psychology Press, 2005) was also a well-written, broad-ranging and informal guide. But as I've argued, the problem of distraction is chiefly one of values and freedom, not psychological or physical detail. Knowing the physiology of attention won't necessarily help us live better, to identify what's important in life and how to attain it.

Most obviously, Friedrich Nietzsche influenced this position. If he was occasionally overzealous or screeching, Nietzsche was nonetheless a brilliant thinker and stylist. Almost everything he wrote, from his first book, *The Birth of Tragedy*, to his last, *Ecce Homo*, contains passages that sparkle, cut and dance. I often recommend *Beyond Good and Evil* to those reading Nietzsche for the first time – it's a radical, imaginative, aggressive book and it leaves a lasting impression of the philosopher at his most daring and endearing. Most of his works are available in fine translations by Penguin, though Cambridge University Press publishes some excellent annotated scholarly translations. I would also recommend the Vintage edition of *The Gay Science* (New York: Vintage, 1974), translated and introduced by Walter Kaufmann. Kaufmann manages to do justice to Nietzsche's finest attributes without being a fawning acolyte. On Nietzsche's life and ideas: Alexander Nehamas's *Nietzsche: Life as Literature* (Cambridge, MA: Harvard University Press, 1985) and R. J. Hollingdale's *Nietzsche: The Man and his Philosophy* (London: Routledge & Kegan Paul, 1965). Carl Pletsch's *Young Nietzsche: Becoming a Genius* (New York: Free Press, 1992) can be rigidly Freudian at times but offers a fascinating portrait of a young scholar cultivating himself.

Robert Musil's brilliant *The Man Without Qualities* (London: Picador, 1995) is well worth purchasing if you can unearth it in a second-hand bookshop. It comes in three volumes and deserves a quiet, sustained read. I bought my first Picador copy in paperback on the advice of a second-hand book dealer (who hadn't read it). I now buy it whenever I can, and pass it on to friends. Milan Kundera's discussion of Musil occurs in *The Art of the Novel* (London: Faber, 1999).

Martin Heidegger's *Being and Time* is one of the great works of the twentieth century – it quite literally changed the way I look at the world. It painstakingly details human relationships with time, things, one another and death. But even in John Macquarrie and Edward Robinson's readable translation (Oxford: Blackwell, 1973), it is a difficult book. A well-written and thoughtful introduction to Heidegger is *Martin Heidegger* by George Steiner (Chicago, IL: University of Chicago Press, 1991). Hubert Dreyfus's *Being-in-the-World* (Cambridge, MA: MIT Press, 1990) is not always for the general reader, but offers a generous, illuminating explanation of Heidegger's magnum opus.

2. What a piece of work is a man

There is a great deal of literature on Karl Marx – much of it dogmatic (on one side or another), or riddled with jargon. To avoid misunderstandings and foggy opinions, it's best to start with the man himself: his *Economic and Philosophical Manuscripts of 1844*. It was written when Marx was younger and less convinced of the "iron clad" science of his economics. In this, it doesn't quite represent how his thought developed in *Das Kapital*, his great three-volume work, available cheaply in a handsome blue Progress Press edition (Moscow: Progress Press, 1977). Still, it's an excellent introduction to some of the basic themes of Marx's philosophy: creative labour, class, alienation and socialism. I greatly enjoyed Francis Wheen's biography of Marx (London: Fourth Estate, 2000) – it's well written, fair and often very funny. I also found Isaiah Berlin's *Karl Marx* (Oxford: Oxford University Press, 1949) helpful, though it lacks Wheen's journalistic verve.

On T. S. Eliot, I was drawn to Peter Ackroyd's *T. S. Eliot* (London: Cardinal, 1981), which gives a nuanced, keen-minded and generous portrait of the great poet. I also learned a great deal from Lyndall Gordon's *Eliot's Early Years* (Oxford: Oxford University Press, 1988) – it gives a charming, intriguing impression of the awkward young Mandarin. Eliot's excellent (and occasionally filthy) letters are collected in *The Letters of T. S. Eliot* (London: Harcourt Brace Jovanovich, 1988), edited by his second wife, Valerie. There is also a wonderful collection of reminiscences on Eliot: *T. S. Eliot: The Man and His Work*, edited by Allen Tate (London: Chatto & Windus, 1967). As for Eliot's own poetry, drama and essays, most are available in Faber editions. A good selection of his literary, political and philosophical opinions can be found in *Selected Prose of T. S. Eliot*, edited by Frank Kermode (London: Faber, 1975).

John Dewey remains an accessible, sensible, helpful writer – precisely the virtues of a so-called "pragmatist". Many of his books deal with the nature of experience; the to and fro between man and world, organism and environment. I'd recommend *Human Nature and Conduct* (New York: Modern Library, 1930) for an introduction to the basics, and *Art as Experience* (New York: Minton, Balch & Co., 1934) for its stunning portrait of creativity in life. Paperback copies of the latter appear in second-hand bookshops regularly – if you're interested in a well-grounded, practical, progressive philosophy of art, it's worth picking up a copy.

Spinoza is also well represented in the second-hand book trade, chiefly in the inexpensive Dover editions: *On the Improvement of the Understanding/The Ethics/Correspondence* (New York: Dover, 1955) and *A Theologico–Political Treatise/A Political Treatise* (New York: Dover, 1951). His *Ethics* is his most notable work, though I particularly enjoyed his correspondence – he gives the impression of a very high-minded, sincere man.

3. The reins of necessity

Alongside Plato, Aristotle is *the* foundational thinker of Western philosophy and science. (In many ways, he was a more rigorous, curious, experimentally minded scholar.) His so-called "virtue ethics" has influenced me greatly (he and Nietzsche are fighting for my soul). Penguin editions of his works are easy to find, with helpful introductions and notes – though Princeton University Press (1984) published an excellent collected works, with classic translations by different scholars. For readers interested in Aristotelian thought, the best works to begin with are his *Nicomachean Ethics* and *Politics* (the second is the practical application of the first). As an elaboration of Aristotle's ideas of necessity, I've drawn on Roberto Calasso's *The Marriage of Cadmus and Harmony* (London: Vintage, 1994), an intriguing, inspiring analysis of myth. An Italian publisher, Calasso is a fine classical scholar, philosopher and literary theorist. All his works reveal a keen, imaginative mind.

On work and technology, I'm indebted to Hannah Arendt's *The Human Condition* (New York: Doubleday, 1959). A student of Heidegger, Arendt's portraits of totalitarianism and mechanical society were astonishingly prescient (far more sociologically penetrating than her teacher's). And her analyses of work, labour and freedom remain relevant half a century on. Nikos Kazantzakis's *England* (Oxford: Cassirer, 1965) is a captivating work of travel writing – it combines philosophical bravura with humane warmth. It also gives a poignant description of Kazantzakis's confrontation with modernity, as spearheaded by the United Kingdom (he never visited America).

Another student of Heidegger, Herbert Marcuse was one of the leading social critics of the post-war period – a rigorous, erudite socialist scholar, unwilling to swallow orthodox Marxist dogma. While prolix at times, his *One Dimensional Man* is a classic analysis of the relationship between society, technology and repression. Hardback copies are easy to find in second-hand shops, and Routledge Classics has a cheap paperback version (but without the retro chic of the 1970s editions).

When he was fashionable (again) in the 1990s, far too much ink was wasted on Heidegger; too many jargon-laden, obscurantist, waffling books and articles (I'm guilty as charged). But there are still some excellent books on Heidegger out there. On his life, Rudiger Safranski's *Martin Heidegger: Between Good and Evil* (Cambridge, MA: Harvard University Press, 1998) is brilliant: a charitable but unfawning portrait of a great thinker. Günther Neske and Emil Kettering's *Martin Heidegger and National Socialism* (St Paul, MN: Paragon House, 1990) is a very helpful resource on the philosopher's politics (Farias's well-known *Heidegger and Nazism* was groundbreaking but ungenerous). The letters between Heidegger and Arendt range from embarrassing to touching and moribund

– I enjoyed them immensely: *Letters: 1925–1975, Hannah Arendt and Martin Heidegger*, edited by Ursula Ludz (New York: Harcourt, 2003). For the curious, Adam Sharr's *Heidegger's Hut* (Cambridge, MA: MIT Press, 2006) offers a fascinating if jargon-laden insight into the Todnauberg retreat. Heidegger's own work on technology is reproduced, along with other seminal essays, in David Farrell Krell's *Martin Heidegger: Basic Writings* (London: Routledge, 1996) – it's an invaluable collection. A good introduction to the sweep of Heidegger's later thought is his *An Introduction to Metaphysics* (New Haven, CT: Yale University Press, 1987), which has some wonderfully dismissive passages on the state of the modern world.

4. A farewell to arms

Machiavelli was an insightful student of history, his own political environment, and human nature – *The Prince* is unflinching and still relevant. It's available in many different editions, new and second-hand (I have a cheap Dover edition). Cornelius Castoriadis's works are excellent reminders of what democracy was for the Greeks and what it deserves to be today. His best essays (including "The Greek *Polis* and the Creation of Democracy") can be found in *The Castoriadis Reader*, edited by David Ames Curtis (Oxford: Blackwell, 1997). His seminal work is *The Imaginary Institution of Society* (Cambridge: Polity, 1997).

Seneca's writings are easy to find – from his tragedies to moral and political works. Penguin publishes most of these, but Oxford University Press and Cambridge University Press also offer well edited and introduced volumes, in readable modern prose. I particularly enjoyed *Letters From a Stoic* (London: Penguin, 2004), which demonstrates Seneca's lucidity, warmth and the charms and challenges of daily life in imperial Rome. On Seneca's life and times, Tacitus's *The Annals of Imperial Rome* (Harmondsworth: Penguin,

1996) offers a dramatic narrative. In *The Twelve Caesars* (London: Penguin, 2003), Suetonius affords a chilling portrait of the Roman aristocracy at its worst. A more modern biography of the statesman and scholar is Paul Veyne's *Seneca: The Life of a Stoic* (London: Routledge, 2002), which also provides a fine explanation of Stoic philosophy and of imperial Rome.

Veyne's friend at the Collège de France, Michel Foucault, was one of the "it" Frenchman of the 1980s and 1990s. He was lauded emptily by many poststructuralist followers and pilloried unfairly by critics on the Right and Left. If his writings lack the systems of Marx (or Bourdieu) or the fastidiousness of historiography, Foucault remains one of the great post-war voices on freedom and power. Even Jürgen Habermas, a strong critic and student of the Enlightenment, said of him: "I just realized how serious he was, how far from the 'circus' he was. I mean, he was a *philosopher*." Some of Foucault's most illuminating essays and interviews can be found in Penguin's *Essential Works of Foucault: 1954–1984* series. His three-volume work on sexuality, *The History of Sexuality* (Harmondsworth: Penguin, 1990), is also a provocative, intriguing read. Of all his writings, I was most impressed by *Fearless Speech* (Los Angeles, CA: Semiotext(e), 2001), a set of lectures on *parrhesia*, or "free speech". Delivered in clear, no-nonsense English, they are a testament to Foucault's courageous, practical thought. On his life, I found James Miller's *The Passion of Michel Foucault* (London: HarperCollins, 1993) invaluable.

A good selection of Bakunin's essays can be found in *Michael Bakunin: Selected Writings* (London: Cape, 1973), edited by Arthur Lehning. *The Political Philosophy of Bakunin* (New York: Free Press, 1953), edited by G. P. Maximoff, has chopped and changed Bakunin's scattered writings into a single work. The result is a contrivance, but a useful one: the headings and sections help to organize the great anarchist's thoughts. Both have short biographical essays. The standard biography of Bakunin remains *Michael Bakunin* by E. H.

Carr (London: Macmillan, 1975), though more recent works are also available. Given the conflicts and tensions between Bakunin and socialists, Carr's work treads a very fine line between generosity and critique. If the revolutionary appears clumsy and impetuous in Carr's work, he also seems sincere, affectionate and intelligent – a noble character, if a tragically flawed one.

Alfred North Whitehead's *Adventures of Ideas* (Cambridge: Cambridge University Press, 1933) is nothing less than a philosophical portrait of Western civilization. It is a worthy addition to any intellectual library and deserves to be standard reading in every philosophy class. Whitehead's witty, intelligent conversations with his wife, friends and colleagues are recorded in *Dialogues of Alfred North Whitehead* (London: Max Reinhardt, 1954) by Lucien Price. My advice on Whitehead is simple: if you see his works in a bookshop, buy them. John Stuart Mill's books and essays are readily available in paperback and hardback – the Everyman editions are hardy, well-sized and easy to read. Mill's *Autobiography* (Oxford: Oxford University Press, 1940) is a compelling, well-written self-portrait. Though not without blind spots, it's an intriguing glimpse into his "inner life" and the struggle to cultivate character. For various perspectives on his life, ideas and legacy, the *Cambridge Companion to Mill* (Cambridge: Cambridge University Press, 1998), edited by John Skorupski, is particularly good (generally speaking, these "companion" titles are excellent resources).

5. Matisse's hernia

The starting point for any work on Matisse is Hilary Spurling's magnificent two-volume biography: *The Unknown Matisse* (London: Hamish Hamilton, 1998) and *Matisse: The Master* (London: Hamish Hamilton, 2005). There are simply too many superlatives to describe Spurling's effort: if you're interested in the painter or the relationship between art and life, these books are priceless. A shorter, less-ambitious but excellent work on Matisse is *Side by Side* (Sydney: Duffy & Snellgrove, 2002) by Sebastian Smee. It gives an even-handed, aesthetically lucid portrait of Matisse, Picasso and their fraught professional and personal relationship. On the same topic, François Gilot's *Matisse and Picasso: A Friendship in Art* (New York: Doubleday, 1990) has some lovely reminiscences. Matisse's works can be found in many city art museums, and reproduced in countless posters. For excellent colour plates at home, I bought Gilles Neret's *Matisse* (New York: Taschen, 1999). For Matisse's own opinions (and those of many other artists and critics), Herschel Chipp's *Theories of Modern Art* (Berkeley, CA: University of California Press, 1969) is a helpful resource.

Marcuse's *The Aesthetic Dimension* (Boston, MA: Beacon Press, 1978) is a small book with a dull title. But it's a brilliant work of philosophy and art appreciation – it demonstrates the vitality of Marcuse's intelligence and artistic sensibility.

Proust's masterpiece, *Remembrance of Things Past* (also translated as *In Search of Lost Time*) is available in several translations and editions. I've used a very large, unwieldy, beautiful edition published by Chatto and Windus (1982), which I gave to my wife, Ruth, as a birthday gift. On Proust's life and work, there are some excellent studies, including: Jean-Yves Tadie's *Marcel Proust: A Life* (London: Viking, 2000), Edmund White's concise *Proust* (London: Weidenfeld & Nicolson, 1999) and Richard Barker's *Marcel Proust* (London: Faber, 1958). Proust's epistles are collected in *Letters of Marcel Proust* (New York: Helen Marx Books, 2006), edited and translated by Mina Curtiss. For fun, William Howard Adams and Paul Nadar's *A Proust Souvenir* (London: Weidenfeld & Nicolson, 1984) is a glimpse of the faces behind Proust's characters, with plenty of photos.

Pierre Bourdieu's *Distinction: A Social Critique of the Judgement of Taste* (London: Routledge, 1996) remains the standard for the sociology of art and culture. Bourdieu's sophisticated writings illuminate academia, education and gender, always with an eye to the everyday signs of class and status. To my mind, his most engaging book is *Pascalian Meditations* (Cambridge: Polity, 2000), which is a brilliantly self-aware work of sociology, psychology and philosophy. Many of his other studies and theoretical tomes are published by Polity and are available second-hand.

Friedrich Schiller's *On the Aesthetic Education of Man* (Oxford: Oxford University Press, 1967) is an uplifting, philosophically daring work. For anyone interested in investigating the edifying power of art, it is an indispensible book. The Oxford, bilingual volume is not easy to find cheaply, but Dover publishes a good, inexpensive edition.

Nikos Kazantzakis's travel memoir *Japan, China* (New York: Simon & Schuster, 1963) is another evocative, enlightening work. If his reflections are occasionally marred by Orientalism, they are also records of his intense philosophical and personal engagement with "the east".

6. The private life

Henry James's prose works are available in many cheap editions, retail and second-hand. Among recent editions, I prefer the typesetting and layout of the Penguin paperback editions. For a taste of his writing, without having to gorge on the entire Lucullan feast of his novels, *Selected Short Stories* (Harmondsworth: Penguin, 1975), edited by Michael Swann, is a good start. Some of his exhaustive, exhausting reviews can be found in *Henry James: Selected Literary Criticism* (Cambridge: Cambridge University Press, 1981), edited by Morris Shapira. "Is There a Life After Death?" appears in *Henry James on Culture* (Lincoln, NE: University of Nebraska Press, 1999), edited by Pierce Walker (other essays in the volume include James's famous piece on the manners of American women). A good collection of his articulate, singular correspondence appears in *Henry James: Selected Letters* (Cambridge, MA: Harvard University Press, 1987), edited by Leon Edel. Edel is also the author of the magnificent biography *Henry James: A Life* (London: Flamingo, 1996). A revised, condensed edition of Edel's five-volume masterwork, this is a beautifully written, painstakingly researched story. I enjoyed it immensely, often alongside James's own works. Colm Toibin's *The Master* (London: Picador, 2006) wears its learning lightly, and it is a wonderful work of factual fiction. If you have to read one book on James's life, pick up a copy of Toibin.

William James's essays are always a joy to read – concise, thoughtful, funny. Many of his popular articles are in *The Will to Believe* (London: Longmans, Green & Co., 1917). *The Principles of Psychology* is easy to find in the Britannica "Great Books" series, though Dover publishes a cheap paperback copy. The abridged edition, entitled *Psychology: A Briefer Course*, is also available from Dover Publications (New York, 2001). For anyone interested in James's adventures in the paranormal, *Essays in Psychical Research* (Cambridge, MA: Harvard University Press, 1986) is a must-read. Despite the seemingly wacky subject matter, James is down to earth, straightforward and scientific. On James's life, I found Linda Simon's *Genuine Reality: A Life of William James* (New York: Harcourt, Brace & Company, 1998) very illuminating. It not only charts William's "inner life" but gives a very readable analysis of his family and times. Henry James's *A Small Boy and Others* (New York: Turtle Point Press, 2001) gives a patchy, sometimes long-winded, occasionally absorbing sketch of his brother and himself as children – no doubt William would have loathed it, lovingly.

Index

Adams, Henry 26
Adventures of Ideas (Whitehead) 86–7, 169
advertising 32, 40
"Advice to a Young Tradesman" (Franklin) 29
Aeschylus 50
The Aesthetic Dimension (Marcuse) 101, 170
aesthetics 101–10, 115, 120, 123
Afghanistan 69
afterlife 150
alienation of labour 15
Allen, Woody 12–13
The Ambassadors (James) 139, 150
Ananke (Necessity) 49–50, 52–3, 57, 60
anarchy 80–85
Anderson, Hendrik 136–7
The Annals of Imperial Rome (Tacitus) 167
Antifa movement 82
anti-Semitism 118–20
anti-sexual instinct 141–3
Arabian Nights 89
architecture 121–2; *see also* art
Arendt, Hannah 50, 58, 118, 166–7
Aristophanes 66
Aristotle 17, 49–52, 61, 91, 116, 124, 165
art 93–4, 96, 98–104, 121–3, 127–8; and Being 121–4; and class 107–10; disturbing 115; galleries 104, 108, 109, 114; impure 157; as an industry 124–5; obstacles to appreciation 104–12, 125–6; openness to 125–6; both sensuous and intellectual 113; *see also* architecture; literature
Art as Experience (Dewey) 34, 165
The Art of the Novel (Kundera) 163
atheism 27, 96
Athens 66–7
attention 1–2
Attention, Perception and Memory (Styles) 162
Australia 82
Autobiography (Mill) 169

Bakunin, Mikhail 80–86, 89, 96, 135, 159, 168–9
Balbec 106–7, 108, 111–12
Bananas 12–13
beauty 113
Beauvoir, Simone de 34
Beethoven, Ludwig van 96
Being 57, 117–19, 121–4, 159
Being and Time (Heidegger) 58, 61, 117, 163
Being-in-the-World (Dreyfus) 163
Belinsky, Vissarion 84
Bentham, Jeremy 90–95
Berlin, Isaiah 164
Beyond Good and Evil (Nietzsche) 162
Bildung 87–90, 94, 96
Bin Laden, Osama 69
The Birth of Tragedy (Nietzsche) 162
Black Forest 58
The Black Tulip (Dumas) 39
BlackBerry 47–8
books, buying 161–2
boredom 26
Borg (*Star Trek*) 60–61

173

bottleneck, single channel 2
Bourdieu, Pierre 107–10, 170–71
British East India Company 90, 92, 94
Brittany 106–7
bullying 31
"Burnt Norton" (Eliot) 8
Burrus, Sextus Afranius 72
Bush, George W. 69
Byron, Lord 94

Calasso, Roberto 50, 165–6
Caligula 72
Calvinism 24–5, 26
Camus, Albert 127
capitalism 18, 118; and asceticism 26–7
Carr, E. H. 83, 84, 168–9
Cartier-Bresson, Henri 82
Castoriadis, Cornelius 65–8, 70, 167
Catholicism 26
chance 145
chaos 9, 19, 27
character 75, 80
charis 159
children 1–2, 43–4
Chomsky, Noam 82
Christianity 26, 51, 78; and work 21–5
churches 78
class 59; and art 107–10
Cold War 83
Coleridge, Samuel Taylor 92
Collingwood, R. G. 124
commitment 13
common sense 116
Commonwealth 81
communication 68–9, 153
communism 18–19, 79, 82–3, 118
community 91
computers 55
conscience 11, 60–62
A Contribution to a Critique of Political Economy (Marx) 14
conversation 9
creative labour/work 16, 18, 28, 37
culture 87–8
curiosity 43

The Dance (Matisse) 102

death 8, 39, 73, 75–6, 102, 131–2, 150, 158, 163
debate 123
democracy 18, 65–71, 78
depression 96
Der Spiegel 120
Descartes, René 39
Dewey, John 33, 34–5, 164–5
dictatorship, of the proletariat 18–19
"The Dilemma of Determinism" (James) 144
discipline 28, 43
Discourses on Livy (Machiavelli) 64
Distinction (Bourdieu) 107–8, 170–71
distraction (defined) 2–5
domestic labour 17
domesticity 36
Don Quixote 89
Dumas, Alexander 39

Ecce Homo (Nietzsche) 162
Economic and Philosophical Manuscripts of 1844 (Marx) 15, 164
economy 18
Edel, Leon 131–2, 134, 135, 142, 172
egotism 159
Einstein, Albert 37
election campaigns 68
Eliot, T. S. 8, 20–24, 26, 27, 28, 33, 158, 164
Eliot, Vivien 20–23
Eliot's Early Years (Gordon) 164
email 31–2, 47–8, 60, 153
emancipation 4, 80
emotion 93
Engels, Friedrich 14, 84
England (Kazantzakis) 53, 166
entrepreneurialism 28
Epicurus 91
Ethics (Spinoza) 40–41, 165
Euripides 66
experience 33
exploitation 28
Expressionism 104

Fabricius, J. Ludwig 38, 39
Facebook 47

Index

factories 53
fallenness 7, 10–11
Fascism 82, 122; see also Nazism
Faster (Gleick) 31
fear 64–5
Fearless Speech (Foucault) 168
feminism 96
femtoseconds 31
film 10, 60
flexible working 32
Forms (Platonic) 157
Foucault, Michel 77–80, 86, 168
Frankfurt School 101
Franklin, Benjamin 29–30, 33
free time 74, 95
freedom (liberty) 4, 13, 16, 35, 40–41, 67, 77, 80, 144–50, 159; and anarchy 81; and democracy 70
Freiburg University 57, 116, 118
friendship 23, 130–31, 154–6; online 10, 154–5
fulfilment 19, 35

Galileo Galilei 51–2, 54
gardening 56
Gates, Bill 48
The Gay Science (Nietzsche) 163
Gemeinschaft 87
gender 59
German Romanticism 88–9
Germany 118–19
Gestell 117–18
Gibbens, Alice 143
Gleick, James 31
God 146
Goethe, Johann Wolfgang von 3, 123
The Golden Bowl (James) 138
government 64–8; 80–81; participation in 68, 70–71
governmentality 78
gratitude 159–60
Greece 45–7
Greer, Germaine 82
Guardian 7, 47
guilt 22, 27, 36

Habermas, Jürgen 168
happiness 41, 91–4
health 36, 126–7, 159

hedonism 146
Hegel, G. W. F. 37, 52, 83, 124
Heidegger, Martin 7–8, 10–11, 61–2, 115–17, 121–6, 159; books on 120, 163, 166–7; Nazism 118–21; on technology 56–9
Herder, Johann Gottfried 88
Hesiod 121
History of Greece (Mitford) 89
History of Sexuality (Foucault) 168
Hitler, Adolf 118–20
HIV/AIDS 79
Hobbes, Thomas 81
Hölderlin, Friedrich 121
Homage to Catalonia (Orwell) 82
Homer 45, 121
Hughes, Robert 102
The Human Condition (Arendt) 166
Human Nature and Conduct (Dewey) 35, 165
Humboldt, Wilhelm von 87–9
Hurricane Katrina 69–70
Husserl, Edmund 118
Huxley, Aldous 20

idealism 99
illness 33, 98–9, 105
The Imaginary Institution of Society (Castoriadis) 167
imagination 93, 157
Impressionism 108
Industrial Revolution 30
industry 28; ownership of 18–19
information 31–2, 153
instrumentalism 117–18
intellect 112–13
internet 10–11, 47, 153
intimacy 154–6
"Intimations of Immortality" (Wordsworth) 94
An Introduction to Metaphysics (Heidegger) 57, 116, 118, 167
iPods 10, 48, 62
Iraq 69
Italian Journey (Goethe) 123
Ithaca 45–7

James, Henry 129–41, 146–55, 171
James, William 140–50, 172

Japan, China (Kazantzakis) 171
Jaspers, Karl 119
Jesus 71
Johnson, Mark 68
Judaism 50–51

Kant, Immanuel 37, 52
Das Kapital (Marx) 83, 164
karate 63
Kaufmann, Walter 163
Kazantzakis, Nikos 53, 126–8, 166, 171
Kundera, Milan 5, 163

labour; Marxist theory 15–18; payment for 29–30; *see also* work
Lakoff, George 68
language 87
laptops 48
laziness 14
Leibniz, Gottfried Wilhelm 37
letters 136, 153, 166–7
liberty *see* freedom (liberty)
lifts 55
literature 5, 34, 129–53, 161
lobbying 67–8
Locke, John 81
loneliness 26, 36, 149
love 64–5, 135, 140–42, 150, 152
love letters 136
Love Song of J. Alfred Prufrock (Eliot) 20, 23
Lucilius 73–6
luxury 108

Machiavelli, Niccolo 64–5, 68, 70–71, 80, 167
machines 47–52
Das Man 8
The Man Without Qualities (Musil) 5–8, 163
Marcuse, Herbert 54–5, 57–8, 100–103, 120, 123, 166, 170
Marmontel, Jean-François 92
marriage 20–21
The Marriage of Cadmus and Harmony (Calasso) 165
Marx, Karl 9, 14–18, 27, 28, 33, 79, 81–4, 164

The Master (Toibin) 131, 172
mastery, over oneself 77–8
mathematics 6
Matisse, Henri 34, 98–104, 135, 158, 169–70
The Matrix 60
Medea (Euripides) 66
medicine 78
metaphors 68–9
Metaphors We Live By (Lakoff & Johnson) 68–9
Mexico 82
Mill, James 89–90, 93–4
Mill, John Stuart 88–97, 159, 169
Miro, Joan 34
mobile phones 46–8, 153
modernism 152
"A Modest Enquiry into the Nature and Necessity of Paper Currency" (Franklin) 29
monarchy 64–5
mortality 8, 157
mothers 17
motivation 148
MP3 players 47
museums 109–10; *see also* art galleries
Musil, Robert 5–7, 163
MySpace 47

National Gallery (London) 104
nature 15–16
Nazism 7, 118–20, 122–3
necessity 49–50, 55
Nehamas, Alexander 163
Nero (Roman Emperor) 72–3, 75
New England Courant 29
New Orleans 70
New York Times 10
Nicomachean Ethics (Aristotle) 165
Nietzsche, Friedrich 4–5, 7, 11, 12, 30, 37, 43, 159, 162–3; on Mill 93, 96
Nobel Prize 127
noise 9–10, 59, 62, 109, 115
North Korea 82
Norton, Grace 134, 147
novels 152

Odyssey (Homer) 45
On Liberty (Mill) 88, 95–6

On Reading (Proust)   105
On the Aesthetic Education of Man
   (Schiller)   112–14, 171
On the Improvement of the
   Understanding (Spinoza)   40–41
"On the Shortness of Life" (Seneca)
   74
One Dimensional Man (Marcuse)   54,
   101, 166
online browsing   *see* internet
"Origin of the Work of Art"
   (Heidegger)   121
Orwell, George   82
otium   74, 95
overtime   33

Paestum   121–2, 123–4
painting   98–102, 111
A Pair of Shoes (Van Gogh)   58
Palm Pilot   47
parenthood   17, 20
Paris Commune   81
Paris VIII, University of   79
parrhesia   168
Pashler, Harold   162
peer recognition   20
Pepys, Samuel   11
Phaedrus (Plato)   159
philosophos   116–17
philosophy   40, 74–5
physis   122
Plato   91, 124, 157–9
play   113–14
pleasure   41
A Pluralistic Universe (James)   149
poetry   21, 34, 121
polis   66–7
political metaphors   68–9
political parties   67, 70
politicians   77–8
politics   64–8, 73–4
Politics (Aristotle)   49, 165
The Portrait of a Lady (James)   139
Post-Impressionism   102–3
poverty   28, 94, 146
pragmatism   149, 164
presenteeism   33
The Prince (Machiavelli)   64–5, 70,
   167

The Principles of Psychology (James)
   140, 144, 148, 172
prisons   78, 81
Prix d'honneur de dissertation de
   France   110
productivity   20, 28, 34
profit   36
proletariat, dictatorship of   81
Prometheus Bound (Aeschylus)   50
propaganda   70
The Protestant Ethic and the Spirit of
   Capitalism (Weber)   24
Protestantism   22–3, 24–5; ascetic
   25–6
Proust, Marcel   104–12, 125, 158, 170
psychology   24, 144
The Psychology of Attention (Pashler)
   162
publishing   161
pubs   9
Puritanism   25, 26, 28, 141

quietism   111, 120, 144

race   59, 82
Realpolitik   70, 73
"The Rectorate 1933/34: Facts and
   Thoughts" (Heidegger)   120
Remembrance of Things Past (Proust)
   106–9, 111–12, 125, 170
Republican Party   69
responsibility   8
rhythms   34–5, 55–6
Ricardo, David   89
rights   70, 78
Rilke, Rainer Maria   121
Romanticism   56, 59, 94, 99
Rome   71
The Rose Marble Table (Matisse)   100
Rothko, Mark   109
routines   34–5
Russell, Bertrand   21
Russia   82–3

Schiller, Friedrich   112–14, 157, 171
Schopenhauer, Arthur   161
science   6, 116
science fiction   60
self, care of   77–9

self-realization 87
Seneca, Lucius Annaeus 71–7, 79, 81, 86, 96, 158, 167
senses 2
Sérusier, Paul 103
servants 17
sex 23, 48, 157
sexuality 79, 137–9, 141–3
Shakespeare, William 121
Shchukin, Sergei 102
shyness 141
slaves 50, 53
A Small Boy and Others (James) 172
Smee, Sebastian 170
Smiley, Jane 6–7
social contract 81
socialism 18–19, 96
socializing 16
sociology 116
Socrates 73
solitude 152
speed 12
Spinoza, Benedict de 37–42, 159, 165
Spurling, Hilary 169–70
standing reserve 57
Star Trek 60–61
State 80–81, 95
status 36
Steiner, George 120, 163
Stoicism 76–7, 78, 93–4
subjectivism 146
Suetonius 72, 168
Sunflowers (Van Gogh) 104

Tacitus 73
technology 10–11, 47–62; of the self 77
television 62
terror 65
text messages 153
theatre 29, 127
Theses on Feuerbach (Marx) 15
Third Reich 119
thought, habits of 101
Thus Spoke Zarathustra (Nietzsche) 43
time 34, 59, 74; and money 29–31; saving 35; standardization of 30

Todnauberg 58
Toibin, Colm 131, 172
totalitarianism 166
trade, free 94–5
traffic 9
truth, "with baggage" 7–8
Turgenev, Ivan 134, 146
The Twelve Caesars (Suetonius) 168
Twilight of the Idols (Nietzsche) 4–5

Unitarianism 22, 26
Untimely Meditations (Nietzsche) 12
utilitarianism 90–95
utopianism 27

value 3–4
Van Gogh, Vincent 58, 104
Veyne, Paul 168
Vietnam 82
virtue ethics 165
voyeurism 144, 146

Wagner, Richard 83
Walpole, Hugh 136, 137, 148
war 64, 81, 146; as a metaphor 69–70
web *see* internet
Weber, Max 24–7, 28–9, 87
Weil, Adèle 105–6
Westminster Review 90
Wharton, Edith 134
Wheen, Frances 164
Whitehead, Alfred North 86–7, 157, 169
Wilde, Oscar 138
The Will to Believe (James) 172
wisdom, love of 116
Woolf, Virginia 129–30, 134, 152, 162
Woolson, Constance Fenimore 130–34
Wordsworth, William 94
work 10, 32, 166; and freedom 41–2; as ennobling 28; motivation for 20, 21–5, 27; rewards of 35, 153–4
working mothers 17
World War II 22
writing 149

YouTube 62